THE POETRY TRIALS

HAMPSHIRE & SUSSEX

Edited by Jenni Bannister

First published in Great Britain in 2016 by:

Remus House
Coltsfoot Drive
Peterborough
PE2 9BF
Telephone: 01733 890066
Website: www.youngwriters.co.uk

All Rights Reserved
Book Design by Ashley Janson
© Copyright Contributors 2015
SB ISBN 978-1-78624-057-6
Printed and bound in the UK by BookPrintingUK
Website: www.bookprintinguk.com

FOREWORD

Welcome, Reader!

For Young Writers' latest competition, *The Poetry Trials*, we gave secondary school students nationwide the challenge of writing a poem. They were given the option of choosing a restrictive poetic technique, or to choose any poetic style of their choice. They rose to the challenge magnificently, with young writers up and down the country displaying their poetic flair.

We chose poems for publication based on style, expression, imagination and technical skill. The result is this entertaining collection full of diverse and imaginative poetry, which is also a delightful keepsake to look back on in years to come.

Here at Young Writers our aim is to encourage creativity in the next generation and to inspire a love of the written word, so it's great to get such an amazing response, with some absolutely fantastic poems. It made choosing the winners extremely difficult, so well done to *Anthony Baillie-Powell* who has been chosen as the best in this book. Their poem will go into a shortlist from which the top 5 poets will be selected to compete for the ultimate Poetry Trials prize.

I'd like to congratulate all the young poets in *Poetry Trials - Hampshire & Sussex* - I hope this inspires them to continue with their creative writing.

Jenni Bannister

Editorial Manager

CONTENTS

Olaide Oni (13) 1
Rosie Day (12) 2
Felicity Guimaraes (14) 3
Esme Scheherazade Heller Golding (11) 4

Brighton Hill Community School, Basingstoke
Sheena-Jean Georgina Dell (11) 4
Oliver Kiff (11) 5
Bradley Taylor (11) 5
Freddie Woods (11) 5

Chamberlayne College For The Arts, Southampton
Ryan Maidment (15) 6

Davison High School For Girls, Worthing
Emma Robinson (14) 7
Cerys Farrell (13) 8
Gabby Rivera Marana (14) 9
Sharon Nwobi (14) 10

Eggar's School, Alton
Liz Puddick (14) 11
Charlotte Francesca Buxton (11) 12
Lily Thirkell (11) 13
Martha Kingsley (14) 14
Molly Hicks (11) 15
Josie Morris (14) 15
Poppy Rowe (11) 16
Callum Stevens (14) 16
Tom William Cowley (14) 17
Zach Harrison (14) 17
Leah Foulds (15) 18
Ansa Sunil (14) 18

Felpham Community College, Bognor Regis
Jasmine Coppock (12) 19
Amber Hayward (12) 20
Megan Tanswell (13) 21
Ting Yang (12) 21

Gildredge House, Eastbourne
Jessica Ray (14) 22
Romilly Huxley (14) 23
Madeleine Horta-Hopkins (11) 24
Saskia Antonia Seguin (11) 25
Estelle Dunton (11) 26
Charlotte Erskine (12) 26

Hurstpierpoint College, Hassocks
Ben Triggs (11) 27
Tabby Woodhams (13) 27
Lydia Firth (12) 28
Emily Coates (11) 28

Ifield Community College, Crawley
Emel Gildir (11) 29
Keira Bethlee Gillett (11) 30
William Campbell-Salmon 31
Inês Isabel Dos Santos Cardoso (12) 32
Sara Chiguer (13) 33
Grace Winnie Brokenshire (13) 34
Chloe-Elise Milborrow (12) 35
Josh Knight-Patto (11) 35
Rebecca Beagles (11) 36
Tia Djelassi (12) 36
Chloe Rowland (11) 37
Jack Robinson (12) 37
Wiktoria Wloszek (11) 38
Jahmelya Muthen (11) 38
Thebekshan Raguraj (11) 39
Ellis Robert Lawrence (12) 39
Katie Heuser (11) 40
Piper Djelassi (12) 40
Lily-Pearl Kirby (12) 41
Maisy Torrington (12) 41
Kayleigh Cumming (12) 42
Yasmine Apps (12) 42
Annie-Louise Thomas (12) 43
Michael Ellis (12) 43
Migle Vasiliauskaite (12) 44
Libby Bradbury (12) 44

Georgia Ryan (11).................. 45
James Loader (11) 45
Tanya Shelby Megan Moore (12).............. 46
Cameron Licence (14)................ 46
Maeve Hona Slocombe (11) 47
Alice Giddings (12)................ 47
Chloe Madureira-Ward (12) 48
Hannah Flint.................. 48
Morgan Rose Sladovich (11) 49
Joshua Ansfield (11) 49
Caitlin Hollis (12)................ 50
Mason Jones (12)................ 50
Poppy Honey Wright (11) 51
Grace Owen (11)................ 51
Sophie Davis-Lyons (13) 52
Abdul Sidhom (12)................ 52
Morgan Scanlon Snell (11) 53
Toby Russell O'Reilly (11)............ 53
Andre Dos Santos (11)................ 54
Tilly Leigh Fewtrell (12)................ 54
Habibah Ahmed (12) 55
Megan Boswell (13) 55
Kai Dwyer (12)................ 56
Mohammed Rahman (11)................ 56
Joel Peacock (11)................ 56
Charlie Marshall Miller (11) 57
Nabil Mehmood (11)................ 57
Amelie Kenvin (12)................ 57
Nitharshika Gnanachandran (11) 58
Nieve Jorgensen Smallwood (11)......... 58
Ricardo Lima Castaneda (12)............ 58

King's School, Brighton
Harrison Coughlan (13) 59
Aiden Perrin (13) 59
Charlotte Wills (13)................ 60
Skye Leonie Collacott Williamson (13)...... 61
Xenia Howard (13)................ 62

Oriel High School, Crawley
Annabell Claire Agate (15).............. 62
Jacob Stephen Cooper (14) 63

Ratton School, Eastbourne
Jazzmyn Ella Young (11) 63
Aisling Nevill (14)................ 64
Abbie Lauren Windham (15)............ 65
Jake Worrell (15)................ 66

Amy Bleach (12)................ 67
Freddie George Cullen (11)............ 67
Kia Howell (14)................ 68
Lynette Riley (12)................ 68
Maggie Rayner (11)................ 69

St George Catholic College, Southampton
Dominic Bakker (13)................ 69
Anthony Baillie-Powell (13) 70
Alec Mills (13) 71
Jeswin Kallukaran (12)................ 72
Kenneth Cacacho (13)................ 72
Ben Patrucco (13)................ 73
Matthew Wilson Levy (13) 73
Patrick James Goodwin (12) 74
Joshua Corry (13)................ 74
Ranjit Landa (12)................ 75

St Paul's RC College, Burgess Hill
Katherine White (14)................ 75
Kate Veronica Brown (11)............ 76
Sam Bouckaert (13)................ 77
Helena Walasek (12)................ 78
Sam Johnson (13) 79
Catty Broz (13)................ 80
Thomas O'Connor (11)................ 81
Josh Mustafa (13)................ 82
Erin Griffin (12) 82
Kaitlin Teresa Grace Griffin (13)............ 83
Callum Smith (13)................ 83
Ella Rose Peck (12)................ 84
Guy Batt (13)................ 85
Alexandra Baker (14)................ 86
Connor Tavener (13)................ 86
Ben Saunders (13)................ 87
Ethan Sumner (12)................ 87
Macy Phillips (13)................ 88
Henry Tomkins (11)................ 88
Niamh Bridger (13)................ 89
Lucy Amerio (12) 89
Niamh Gallagher (13)................ 90
Lily Rooney (13)................ 91
Joseph Carter (12)................ 92

The Angmering School, Littlehampton

Caitlin Roberts (16) 92
Marcus Nicholas Bird (16) 93
Liam Gilbey (17) 94
Jack Chapman (12) 95
Charlie James Douglas Batchelor (18) 96
Louis Haste (16) 97
Jasmine Payne (12) 98
Ben Simpson (17) 99
Chloe Paisley (14) 100
Sophie Baker (14) 101
Toby Hother (14) 101
Amy Wilson (11) 102
Sophie Wayman (11) 102
Emma Needle (11) 103
Lily Tamara Wells (12) 103
Jagoda Iwanska (11) 104
Alex Furniss (11) 104
Thomas Hartigan (11) 105
Oliver Fullbrook (11) 105
Holly Parisi (16) 106

The Costello School, Basingstoke

Isabel Cosgrove (12) 106
Charlotte Rebecca Hill (15) 107
Taine Macleod Peacock (14) 108
Charlotte Harfield 109
Millicent Crass (14) 110
Freya Barter (12) 111
Ryan Baker (11) 112
Amy Regan 113
Katie Jeffery 114
Alex Danylyuk (14) 115
Hugh Sergeant 116
Harrison Keast (11) 117
Phoebe Mahoney (11) 118
Joe Duerden (14) 119
Natalie Gay 120
Thomas Barton (11) 120
Isobel Reid (11) 121
Elliot Turner (12) 121
Callum McKeaveney 122
Ben Matthews (14) 122
Kaviya Balasritharan 123
Erin Onel Edgar (12) 124

Amy Kent (11) 125
Chelsea-Marie Cochrane 126
Erica Van Den Ordel (15) 126
Delia Gheorghe 127
Keira Purver (11) 127
Megan Temple-Nidd (12) 128
Brioni Fayter 128
Ollie Pegg 129
Becki Giggs 129
William Colegate 130
Alexander De Silva (11) 130

The Forest School, Horsham

Harrison Konieczny (12) 131
Nathan Kettle 132
David Ironmonger 132

The Gregg School, Southampton

Rachael Locke (12) 133
Holly Beadsworth (12) 134
Emily Kerry (13) 135
Henry Gates (11) 136
Alice Dowling (12) 137
Abby Hanslip (11) 137
Lillie Bishop (11) 138
Patrick Berry (11) 138
Samuel Matthew Jenkins (12) 139
Megan Margereson (11) 139
Hannah Creighton (11) 140
Millie Law (13) 140
Rosie Boxall (11) 141
Mitch Soper (11) 141
Evelyn Hall (11) 142
Edward Shipley (11) 143
Elliott Oldrey (11) 144
Kaira Feyerabend-Powell (12) 144
Alexander Charlton (11) 145
Jake Smoker (12) 145
Daniel Jones (11) 146
Will Nelson-Smith (11) 146
Chloe Grace Errington (12) 147
Ollie Mossman (12) 147
Paloma Charlotte Hoyos (11) 148
Mark Bowman (11) 148
Isobel Bailey (11) 149
Eleanor Wright (11) 149
Ben Cameron (11) 150

Henry Earl (11) 150
Paul Lennon Mills (11) 151
Sarah Hassan (13) 151
Madeline Bennett (11) 152
Anna Houghton (12) 153
Olivia Munro-Martin (13) 153
Georgia Murray (13) 154
Jonathon Duddington (11) 155

The Henry Beaufort School, Winchester

Fifi Palmer (11) 156
Rebecca Jane Tan (11) 157
Ines Mazdon Delas (14) 158
Holly Marshall (11) 159
Eliot Liversidge (12) 160
Keian John Offord (13) 161
Oscar Edward Thompson (11) 162
Laura Arnott (11) 163
Alice Little (11) 164
Amy Justine Offord (12) 165
Tia Burgin (14) 165
Betsy Harvey (11) 166
Astha Subba (12) 166
Rohan May (13) 167
Ben Elkins (12) 168
Ellena Lousie Cable (12) 169
Hannah Louise Woodhall (11) 170

The Towers Convent School, Steyning

Megan O'Neill (13) 170
Megan Viljoen (13) 171
Jemima Coleman (14) 172
Francesca Blondell (13) 173
Ella Savage (13) 174
Freya West (13) 175
Georgia Howarth (13) 176
Maddi Scarborough (13) 176

THE POEMS

THE UNTOLD GENERATION

'Blood, sweat and tears' describes,
What my ancestors thought of their lives, inside.
Crystal tears rested upon their broad, scarred faces.
However, the man only saw the defects as eternal disgraces.
The word: 'worthless'.
Emotionally embedded in their minds;
The dilapidated cat o' nine tails were far more kind.

The servants' mothers and fathers watched in dismay,
As their children were forced to obey
Soon discovering their... 'precious gifts' were impregnated the following day.

'Blood, sweat and tears' describes,
What my ancestors thought of their lives - inside.
A desolate void displaced the man's true heart;
Emotions pierced by an acute dart.
Aspirations lost:
'How much did that cost?'

'Peace,' the man once claimed.
Was it a fantasy?
Was the man sane?
Sacrifice made.
One individual saved.
Stand naive at another's grave.
Every day.
Replay.

Signs of defeat.
Hesitation cannot repair these crippled destinies.
No time to take a seat.
Lest not forget our roots or history may repeat.

'Blood, sweat and tears' describes,
What my ancestors thought of their lives, inside.

Olaide Oni (13)

FIRE WITHIN

No words can convey the fire within,
The pain,
The tears,
The open wounds …

Fire sears through my veins,
Ripping every muscle in two,
The bones splinter in its wake,
The shards lodging themselves into my soft tissue,
Cutting deep.

The poison sets in,
Every nerve tears itself from its neighbour,
It is the only way to free my mind from the torture of life,
The only way to disappear.

My mind burns,
It tenses and strains with every passing second,
Throbbing,
Throbbing.

Violent spasms course through my back and arms,
The pain mauls all feeling but itself into fragments,
Much like Death is clawing at my throat.

Agony.

I let out a howl,
Not even this can subdue the power of the Devil.

The poison reaches my heart,
My mind shoots warning signals out,
My hands fly straight to my neck.

I snatch the last breath I will take in this life,
Then,
Blackness.

Rosie Day (12)

A THOUSAND WORDS

A smile can mean a thousand words,
But sometimes means just one.
Spacious smiles spread happiness,
Stunted smiles oust words,
They bring help to the helpless.
They bring happiness to the sad.
They mean sorry,
And thank you,
And just mean that you're glad.
Glad you're with the people you love,
Or glad you're on your own,
Nevertheless,
A smile can mean a thousand words.

A frown can mean a thousand words,
But sometimes means just one.
It can show disappointment,
Confusion,
And hurt,
Full frowns bring people closer,
And also, tear them apart.
Petty frowns do the same thing,
But are worn with less heart.
Nevertheless,
A frown can mean a thousand words.

Felicity Guimaraes (14)

SORRY, EQUALITY

What is causing this insanity?
Nations have high expectations,
Humanity takes selfies purely for reasons of vanity,
Things that were placed to obstruct are destruct,
A dispute between locals and pinstriped suits,
More accusations of racism,
More black people held at the police station,
A nation drives to insanity,
Sorry, Equality,
This is a sincere apology.

Esme Scheherazade Heller Golding (11)

WHITE IS ...

Snow is a blank start,
A scrub board,
It's harsh and vacant,
In which you wait,
It's a bird, moral and light,
Flying, it can also look damp and lonely,
It's the flavour of pasta and marshmallows
And a touch of books.

Sheena-Jean Georgina Dell (11)
Brighton Hill Community School, Basingstoke

SPACE

When I go to space,
It's like trying something new for the first time,
When you're in that spacecraft,
It's like being in slow motion.
You feel like you're on an adventure,
When you look back on your home,
You think bye for now.

Oliver Kiff (11)
Brighton Hill Community School, Basingstoke

HALLOWEEN

Halloween is fun
Halloween is scary
Halloween is when all the ghouls come out
Halloween is when you get lots of goodies
Halloween is where teenagers wear hoodies.

Happy Halloween (not a scary one).

Bradley Taylor (11)
Brighton Hill Community School, Basingstoke

HALLOWEEN

Pumpkins are orange like oranges,
People are scary like zombies,
Trick or treating's like candy falling
From the dark, spooky sky.

Spiders, creepy like rats
Spreading a gross disease.

Freddie Woods (11)
Brighton Hill Community School, Basingstoke

ASYLUM

As I wander the dark, empty corridors of the asylum that is my mind,
I see all the dark memories,
All that has caused pain and suffering
Locked away in a rusty cell of my thoughts
In the dark asylum that is my mind.

I hear the rattling of my chains,
The fear within the walls.
It waits for no man,
It tries to escape
And if I let it,
I lose all I have ever fought for,
In the dark asylum that is my mind.

As the light dims and the room darkens,
Thoughts arise,
Plotting.
I try my best to forget,
But they never let me
In the dark asylum that is my mind.

Battered and broken,
The rusted cage cannot contain anymore,
The memories so impure they turn the sweetest wine
to ashes in my mouth.
My mind torments me,
It plagues me,
In the dark asylum that is my mind.

Beaten by my memories,
My lifeless brain lies dormant, awaiting sweet release.
There's no escape now,
Battered and broken,
In the dark asylum that is ...
My mind?

Ryan Maidment (15)
Chamberlayne College For The Arts, Southampton

WHY I DON'T WANT A CHILD

I am an abomination;
For I stand with determination,
To never give another respiration,
As to add to our population,
Would be my child's termination.

I refuse to live in a massive hallucination,
To march in the same formation,
Just like those of my generation.
I'm stuck in this location,
Somehow part of a nation,
All of us headed for the same destination.

We abuse and ignore desired information,
To gain a reputation,
In the hopes of prolonged identification,
To be mentioned in someone's future conversation.

They haven't yet made the observation,
That life's nothing but an illustration.
We are fooled as a civilisation,
That we can live without limitations.

Stuck together in the same situation,
Preaching and repeating one's declaration;
That this world isn't going to be our problem,
It will be *theirs*.

I won't let it get to that point though
As I will never give another respiration,
As to add to our population,
Would be my child's termination.

Unless we are able to use a small part of our education,
And a big part of our imagination,
We could create a world of signification.

Emma Robinson (14)
Davison High School For Girls, Worthing

HER GIFT

A bouquet of flames wrapped in my icy hands,
Passing through the home of my childhood.
Leaves falling like snow,
Crunching their song beneath the soles of passers-by.
Colours of fire dancing around me,
Raging and vibrant yet cold as the ocean.

I wish she was here to see this gift.

Scenes of sweet innocence knocking upon doors,
Their facade cute as they scavenged their fellow trickers for treats.
Wearing cloths of bland grey,
Cheeks lit by a dusting of plum.
Wicked-looking plastic allies accompany them on their mission,
Protecting their haul of luminous wrapped sugar.

I wish she was here to see this gift.

A great river of fire made of graceful, rippling flames,
Reflecting me in its shimmering surface
As I glide through this glorious labyrinth of red and gold.
Hovering above the river's touch hangs an old friend,
A cobbled mouth that hangs agape,
His lower lip trembles with the soft ripples of the lake.
The source of movement repelling from a forest creature with such grace,
Silhouetted by the spotlights pouring through the tree's cover,
Lapping at the water and straightening tall and elegant with much pride.

I wish she was here to see this gift.
Up on the hill her willow sits.

Waves of wind hugging her delicate leaves
And tossing them gently from side to side.
Wind rushes over my face, pieces of debris tickle my cheeks,
Breathing the air she gave me.

Beneath it, her stone awaits my company,
A gift of withered love fades at her feet.
Roots of her willow disappear beneath her,
Intertwining with the decay of her home.
For engraved in her loving memory,
My mother made her own gift for others to know.

Cerys Farrell (13)
Davison High School For Girls, Worthing

WHAT HAPPENS AFTER THAT?

You see me in the hallway, standing alone
You come over towards me ever so slow
You ask me if I'm okay and I say I'm fine,
What happens after that?

We see each other often, almost every day,
Almost inseparable I'd like myself to say,
We visit each other's houses each day after school,
What happens after that?

The time we spend together increases more and more,
I've found myself in less of a bore,
You made me feel special when I was with you,
What happens after that?

One day when we were in our secret place together,
You asked me the question and I felt like a feather,
I happily agreed and hugged you close,
What happens after that?

We spend countless hours with each other,
You make me feel alive like no other,
You tell me you love me and I retaliate the words,
What happens after that?

Our peace turned to war a little bit after,
I started to go, made with bitter laughter,
You leave through the door and now we're back to the beginning,
Nothing... happened after that.

Gabby Rivera Marana (14)
Davison High School For Girls, Worthing

SPRING

Awakening to a delightful season,
Fresh sunshine pours down from the sky.
Withheld for a season,
Everyone is thirsty for it.
A real blessing, it whips out
The winter flu from everyone.

Flowers begin to blossom,
Like shiny jewels.
Green leaves spring forth,
From dying trees.
It draws with it many treats,
Like a Santa with a bag of goodies
Though it's not Christmas.
It greets everyone with Easter kisses.

Hedgehogs awake from their slumber.
Birds fill the sky with melodies.
Chocolate eggs and rabbits,
Shared around.
Happiness is written on all faces.
It's the beginning of a new life.
A treasure to both Earth and humanity,
It's spring!

Sharon Nwobi (14)
Davison High School For Girls, Worthing

THE SILENT THIEF

Darkness falls,
And all that's left,
Is street lamps dimmed,
And a silent theft.

But listen to the rain
And the lonely lover's pain,
And you'll see this crime
Is the worst of its kind.

This silent theft,
Creeps in at night,
Crushes dreams
And steals the light.

Jealousy rages,
Love ends,
And this lonely man
Can no longer make amends.

He wants to take
What others gain,
What he himself
Cannot obtain.

So on this cold night,
The thief has wet hair
And as the rain falls,
Many hearts will tear.

Liz Puddick (14)
Eggar's School, Alton

WONDERLAND

(A Lipogram - T)

Mad as a Munchkin
Crazy as a queen
As big a fork in a road
As ever I've seen
A haberdashery full of wonder
A higgledy-piggledy land
Upside down

A pack of cards all over Wonderland
All crazy card soldiers
As wonderful a group as ever I've seen
A wonderlandiful world
A haberdashery full of wonder
A higgledy-piggledy land
Upside down

A crazy girl
Who's always disappearing
A pranking girl
A cheeky girl as ever I've seen
A wonderlandiful world
A haberdashery full of wonder
A higgledy-piggledy land
Upside down.

Charlotte Francesca Buxton (11)
Eggar's School, Alton

THE POETRY TRIALS - HAMPSHIRE & SUSSEX

THE DEADLY ARENA

Darting through the trees,
Hands gripped on my bow,
I spun around and loosed my arrow,
Into the heart of my evil foe.

The boy who camouflaged himself,
The girl who sang with the birds similar to on my pin,
The boy so desperate to survive,
There is no way I can win.

As the fire engulfs me,
In a circle of doom,
I see someone else get trapped,
As the cannon goes boom.

I know I'm going to die here,
Right in this very spot,
But as everything closes in,
The world seems as small as a dot.

When I wake up,
Everything's a blur,
As I sit there waiting, scared,
For the unimaginable to occur.

Lily Thirkell (11)
Eggar's School, Alton

A REPAIR OF A BICUSPID AORTIC VALVE

My wait I passed with lots and lots of films.
Sitting countless times on the bed and someone going over it all again.
Like a rising wave, a sudden nausea and fear because there is no other way.
Blinding light and the cleanness of white
High-pitched sound clashing horrifically (consonance is what is not dissonant)
Like a camera trying to take a picture; in out, in out.
Peace.

My breath doesn't want to support me;
The very subsistence of life stuffed down my throat,
A voice of love over the shout of panic.
Loss of place and time.

A smudge of darkest chocolate,
She wants to help.
Time is a thing that is only measured by itself
When it is lost, what to do but watch the proceedings and measure time.
A soul like any other comes to bid her away,
Leaving all silence but the dynamic discord, unrelenting.

The potion is poison,
Bleeding into my body, doing its heavenly, dirty work.
The thud and pulse of light; I don't need what is needed.
I fear my body is fragile like glass,
If I move, I break, open up.
These endless nights of unfulfilling sleep.
My heart beating, not only for me as it beeps merrily along;
No need to fear.
Radiance, carefree,
Laughing in the bathroom (dissonance is what is not consonant)
Gran being there.
My wait I passed with lots and lots of films.

Martha Kingsley (14)
Eggar's School, Alton

A SECRET CHANGE

Laa, as I sing to the fishes,
Laa, as I sing to the birds above.
They are the only company I have.
I don't know who I was,
I only know who I am.

Nobody remembers me,
I am a myth, a secret.
This is my life, how I want to keep it.

Change can be a good thing,
But only if you want it to be.
I'm not one for change,
But change can't stop;
It keeps going.

I don't want to change,
I love life,
I don't want it to end.

Molly Hicks (11)
Eggar's School, Alton

THESE COLD DAYS

On these cold days,
I sit by the lake,
Watching as the blanket of winter covers nature,
Leaving cold, hard frost in its wake.

These cold days are my most treasured
Because down by the lake it's almost as if
Time has stopped,
Cold, hard, stiff.

All that is heard,
Is the cold, harsh wind through the trees
And the occasional chirping of a bird,
On these cold days.

Josie Morris (14)
Eggar's School, Alton

THIS IS WINTER

Winter is when snow comes,
Kettles boil to keep us cosy,
Snow spikes sit on the pipes,
Children run outside to build snowmen,
Dinner is served on lovely hot dishes.

The fires gush on full power,
Hot drinks with dipped in biscuits,
Dinner served for everybody,
Sledges skid down the hills,
Stockings hung by the chimney,
Frozen toes feel the cold,
The moon glows brightly in the sky,
This is winter!

Poppy Rowe (11)
Eggar's School, Alton

CYCLE OF SEASONS - HAIKUS

Long, green grass growing
Dandelions taking flight
Hot air lifting stress

A cold autumn breeze
Beneath the tunnel of trees
Pierced by sunlight

Breath creating fog
The crunch of my feet echoes
Days running away

Sunflowers blooming
Heat beginning to rise then
English weather comes...

Callum Stevens (14)
Eggar's School, Alton

TIME

Life is like a path,
But where does it lead?
Do we actually know where we will be
In ten years' time?
What we may have seen,
Witnessed, been part of,
Will we be in the same town, country
Or somewhere far off?
Truth is, we can't answer
Any of these questions, for time will tell ...
Will you be rich, famous
Or just another cog in the machine?
Well, have patience, as that remains to be seen.

Tom William Cowley (14)
Eggar's School, Alton

MY BIKE

Pedalling
Wheels turning
Spinning gracefully around
Quicker and faster
Never braking
On and on
Don't stop!
On and on
Braking never
Faster and quicker
Around gracefully spinning
Turning wheels
Pedalling!

Zach Harrison (14)
Eggar's School, Alton

PHOTOGRAPH

A picturesque ambience, its breathtaking artistry
Captured.
Taken from the ordinary, presents to shape and inspire
The emotion gathered.
Virtuous perception, laughter and awestruck with beauty,
Overcome and jubilant,
Viewing it through a new window.
To melancholy, fear striking the senses
Of ambiguous, distressed crowds of overshadow.
Memories locked to be forever examined,
Emotions endlessly flowing.
Adventures cresting, excitement bubbling,
Beauty unleashed until it feels like floating.

Leah Foulds (15)
Eggar's School, Alton

ANOTHER DAY ...

Another day,
Being painted with the colour grey
Another day,
Where the trees start dancing to the music of the wind.
Another day,
Where rain becomes nature's food.
Another day,
Where I hear raindrops patter on the roads.
Another day,
Where the raindrops looked like Mother Earth's tears.

Ansa Sunil (14)
Eggar's School, Alton

BLACK

Black, is as dark as night.
It is fear.
It is a bat flying through the sky.
It darkens our mood, our enemy our food.
We feel desolate, dark and dangerous.
Black corrupts our emotions.

Life's a serpent, twisting and turning.
Black is the death under the grass.
It can be the monster under the bed.
Black is as scary and evil as a villain.
It creeps in our bedrooms, our homes, our minds.

Darkness destroys our trust in friends.
In our family.
In ourselves.
Black slithers inside us.
Eating us from the inside out.

It empties our soul.
Our fears are black.
Our enemies are dark.
Our lives are lonely.
Black is the colour that shows our emotion.
Anger. Fear. Loneliness.
Black tears us down, bit by bit.
Brick by brick.

Black is as dark as your dreams.
Black is unconscious.
But it awakens us.
Turn off the light and what is left?

Jasmine Coppock (12)
Felpham Community College, Bognor Regis

NIGHT

The orange glow of the sunset
Stretching up from the horizon,
Its fingers of flame pulling a curtain of stars across the glass dome sky
Enveloping the Earth into darkness.

The timid waves of a vast sea collapsing onto the sandy shore,
Only to be dragged back again by the moon's haunting glow
That reflected against the liquid mirror.

An explosion of light erupting from the horizon,
Nature's beauty revealing itself.
Orange, yellow, reds and purples lay in the clouds
That sit on top of each other like bricks of a house.

The night holds many secrets and wonders,
Concealed in the darkness,
Never to be known.

Amber Hayward (12)
Felpham Community College, Bognor Regis

THE POETRY TRIALS - HAMPSHIRE & SUSSEX

WHAT IS SHE?

The horse that runs in the air,
The horse that is lightning and thunder,
The horse that has the flaming hooves,
The horse that has the long, gold mane,
The horse that has wings,
The horse that can fly,
The horse that is not a horse at all,
The horse is Pegasus,
Pegasus that has the big, blue eyes,
Pegasus that has the wings of fire,
Pegasus that has the long, flowing tail of gold,
Pegasus that has a horn,
Pegasus is a unicorn,
The unicorn that has the golden horn,
She is the queen.
She is the alicorn.

Megan Tanswell (13)
Felpham Community College, Bognor Regis

BLUE

What is blue?
Blue is the colour of the sky,
Blue is the colour you can't buy,
Blue is the colour of my dreams when I sleep,
Blue is the colour you can always keep,
Blue is the colour of a tear,
Blue is the colour that makes you cheer,
Blue is the colour of wavy seas,
Blue is the colour that's everywhere you can see,
Blue is the colour you can't ever forget.

Ting Yang (12)
Felpham Community College, Bognor Regis

DREAMS

Sometimes the best thing to do is think,
Just think.
Think about your ambitions for the future,
The ones you have aspired to,
Given blood, sweat and tears to achieve.
They are smoke.
Pure smoke.

Always just out of your reach,
Always there.
But you never dream of letting them slip,
Constantly swirling around your head,
Like the mist of a vast forest.
They are seeds.
Emerging seeds.

Seeds yet to blossom, flourish,
Thrive, evolve.
Dream.

Jessica Ray (14)
Gildredge House, Eastbourne

THE POETRY TRIALS - HAMPSHIRE & SUSSEX

LIPOGRAM

(A Lipogram - E)

Miss says to jot down lipograms at school
Glancing at plans, I think it highly uncool
My class all find it slightly fun
Comparisons amongst pals going on
But I? I find it horribly plain,
So I think to purport as highly vain
To turn down all work
And turn up my snout
And if Miss complains, I will kick and shout
And soon my plan is in full swing
I frown at my companions until, slowly
Following suit, many stop writing, until
Just boring swots think about lipograms.
So what my task to drill Miss with is:
Don't assign a boring task, and I
Might think to do it.

Romilly Huxley (14)
Gildredge House, Eastbourne

MOON

The moon is a sliver of light,
Emerging from the darkness of night's unfolding arms.
Its twinkle is a soft glimmer;
Mocking the people as they surface from the dark.

Its sparkling tint is refreshing and crisp
Like the lonely flakes of snow falling on a winter's morning.
It is a hollow circle of light,
Illuminating the coal-black night.

The gentle feel of newly-washed sheets.
The heavy weight of stone.
It vanishes and reappears,
Just to say hello.

After its long slumber as its rival greets the morning,
The moon races out to lighten the night,
Blocking out the willowy shadows
And driving them away,
With one final glare of its bright crystal colour.

It falls back into the sky,
With a light grace of eeriness and mystery.
Its serenading whispers chant the word 'goodbye'.

Madeleine Horta-Hopkins (11)
Gildredge House, Eastbourne

THE POETRY TRIALS - HAMPSHIRE & SUSSEX

SNOWSTORM

Winter days so lonely and sad,
Snow falling down from the fuming, grey clouds
Like there is a storm inside my chest
Beating against my thumping heart
I stare into the snowstorm coming my way
I try to find a way to escape
But there is nowhere to hide.
I'm stuck in a fuming snowstorm
I don't know where to go
I'm lost, so sad, there I stand
Struggling to stick to the ground, to stand still
But I can't.
The fearsome wind pushing me
Wanting me to go flying away to somewhere I don't know
I pray, I hope that I would become a girl
With dreams that no one has ever thought of before.
I want to leave this horrible snowstorm
Someone help me
Before I'm gone.

Saskia Antonia Seguin (11)
Gildredge House, Eastbourne

CLOUDS

Rain falling down as the clouds begin to frown,
Illuminating the sky and releasing a small, wispy cry,
As they chase away the shadows,
Tearing through the skyscraper trees,
Catching on and falling through leaves,
A sleepless night filled with fright.

Drafting apart the empty copper canvas, welcoming the first rays of light,
Serenading the passers-by as they race over the sky, free from any fright,
Wiping away the last dark shadows of the past,
Carried on the wind, lighting the streets with a smile and a laugh.
They have made their final path.

Estelle Dunton (11)
Gildredge House, Eastbourne

STARS

Stars are a natural wonder,
The beauty of the night sky,
They inspire dreams and ambition,
And bring light to the night.

They are the diamonds of space,
A source of hope in an infinite void,
They bring life to darkness,
And power to the loneliest souls.

They are the origins of mythical beings,
They are the magic that powers fairies,
And they shine bright in the deep space,
And into the void beyond.

Charlotte Erskine (12)
Gildredge House, Eastbourne

THE POETRY TRIALS - HAMPSHIRE & SUSSEX

I DON'T WANT TO WRITE MY POEM

I don't want to write my poem,
I'd rather just play with my toys,
Poetry isn't for me,
It's really not something for boys.

Please don't make me do anymore,
I've done all my homework today,
I'm tired of being a good boy,
When can I just stop and play?

I don't want a job as a poet,
There's nothing more boring than writing,
I want to fight ninjas in space,
That would be much more exciting.

So forgive me for failing my task,
But wait, hold on a minute,
I've suddenly realised something,
This is a poem, innit?

Ben Triggs (11)
Hurstpierpoint College, Hassocks

A PEN

A pen can write a story
A pen can tell your tale
A pen can write your shopping list
A pen can do your maths.
We use one,
Throw it away,
Or keep it for another day.
A pen doesn't care
About what you think
Who you're writing to
It just runs its ink.

Tabby Woodhams (13)
Hurstpierpoint College, Hassocks

READING

Open a book, get lost in the words.
A portable travelling life.
Step into situations, or incredible moments.
Not just 'black-and-white-boring' not just 'waste-of-time',
But inspiration, hope and love,
Swirling in your mind.
Unthinkable consequences, believable ups and downs.
A forest to get lost in, the future behind.
A splash of colour in a grey vision,
Receive knowledge, react and become,
Absorbed in the forest,
Trapped in the world,
Of reading.

Lydia Firth (12)
Hurstpierpoint College, Hassocks

THE APPLE TREE

Just beneath the apple tree leaves
Lies the juiciest apple I've ever seen
The redness, the shine, as it lies in the sun
I jump up to reach but it's way too far up
I try one more time but have no luck
So the rest of the day I sit by the tree
I stare up at the apple, that apple's for me
But still with no luck, in the end I give up
But autumn did come and the tree turned bare
My juicy, red apple is no longer there.

Emily Coates (11)
Hurstpierpoint College, Hassocks

LIFE

I turn my face towards the warm night sky,
A tear slipping from my eye;
It feels like my life is slipping away,
Should I be dead or alive?

In the distance I hear a cry.
I long for the day there is nothing but darkness.
I huddle up in my coat,
As I wait for someone who is mine.

Killing myself, I decide
Was the best idea over time,
My family is there, so what to fear,
Today or tomorrow,
I'll be gone

For evermore, forever long.

But again I hear a cry,
And in the distance there was a movement,
I told myself that my mind was playing a game,
Only then I realise who it was in confusion,
But then again I gave them a hug,
Feeling warm again and loved,
I forgave whoever they were, anyways,
They cared for me,
I then never thought of running away,

Just then I realised after all those years,
It was my mother who was there for me when I fell,
And now she was here in my arms ,
And in my mind were bluebells,
No sadness,
Or fear,
All that mattered was that my mother was here.

Emel Gildir (11)
Ifield Community College, Crawley

MY STORY WILL LAST FOREVER

Since the dawn of time I have seen everything,
From the rotten Romans to the ghastly Greeks.
I have seen the birth of the dinosaurs
And also their extinction.
In the past year I have grown immeasurably wide,
My story will last forever.

Every day my body welcomes the warming sun
As it rises,
The orange eye observes me
As I lie below the glowing sunlight.
I sit and watch the dunes slowly move across me,
My sand leaping across my back
And catapulting onto the rocks.
I am cold.
Now I am warm.

As it comes to midday,
My sandy hands cautiously creep up the rocks
To find new people crossing my pale,
Gritty body.
As I become hot,
I start to rage
And I let my anger grow into a blistering sandstorm
That whips.

As my storm dies down,
The heatwaves jump across my rippling body.
I relax.
As the air slowly cools through the hours
I stay calm.
I gently connect my fingertips to your soft feet.
I am still calm,
As the delicate feet of the animals cross me.

The day draws to a close,
All the animals go to bed,
So there is no more scampering on me.
I now start to feel tired,
But I stay awake to explore the night.

Now the wind is icy,
The silence deafens me.
I stare into the sky
And I watch the dark eye of the moon,
Glaring.
The wind makes the sand dance across my back.
The sparkling stars in the sky form perfect constellations,
I imagine them coming alive.

I am danger.
I am safety.
My story will last forever.
I am the desert.

Keira Bethlee Gillett (11)
Ifield Community College, Crawley

CONFLICT

Two sides meet,
One must defeat,
Preparing for war,
Knocking down doors,
Loading weapons,
Preparing to fight,
At the dark of night,
We wait for the signal,
My heart trembles with fear,
My body overwhelmed.

Bang! Bang! The air raids fill the air with explosions,
People dropping dead all over the blood-covered streets,
Tanks firing at planes in the sky.
Bombs flying down onto the ground,
Destroying homes and land.

The war is finally over,
Free from conflict, free from bloodshed.
But is the war truly over?
Will I see my family once more?

William Campbell-Salmon
Ifield Community College, Crawley

IT'S THE DAY OF THE DEAD!

Carved pumpkins drenched in blood,
Children's nightmares just begun,
It's the day of the dead.

Knock, knock, on a wood frame door,
This poor child has no idea what's awaiting her behind the door,
It's the day of the dead.

Smashed windows, haunted halls,
Gory ceilings and mouldy walls,
It's the day of the dead.

Ghoulish paintings hanged and framed,
Is this person really insane?
It's the day of the dead.

A girl's reflection on a bloody, shattered mirror,
A vicious, bloodthirsty demon awaiting its victim,
It's the day of the dead.

A ghostly shadow on the wall,
A haunted car above it all,
It's the day of the dead.

A deathly trail of blood on the floor,
And an unexpected roar behind the door,
It's the day of the dead.

Now my dark painting is complete,
You are in for a treat,
Now, little girl, you must write your murderous notes,
There was no blood and no ghosts,
You have just said my gruesome spell,
Now your life is cursed in Hell,
I told you it was the day of the dead.

Inês Isabel Dos Santos Cardoso (12)
Ifield Community College, Crawley

MY WORLD

A time ago
I knew what the world was . . .

My heart sinks, looking below the soles of my feet
What has the Earth become?
Pieces of glass and rubble fill the land for miles
Pieces of broken memories and hope.

A deserted land of what used to be
A school - an elementary school
I could hear the children
I could just imagine
Children screaming; full of happiness and joy;
Excitement and ambition
The only scream that filled these halls
Were the deafening screams of silence.

The air is dry
Dust brushes across my face
Scorched lands; they're desperate
Desperate for water
Desperate for life
I hear its cry
Nothing but fields of thirst.

Where have my people gone?
I ask myself.
They have been enslaved
By a disease that conquered the world
But only I can find the answer
Only I can terminate this epidemic.

Sara Chiguer (13)
Ifield Community College, Crawley

PEACE ON EARTH

Guns fire,
Fire hard,
No love here,
No love here,
Bombs come crashing down below,
No hearts here,
No hearts here.

See through the young eyes,
Eyes that are still growing,
Eyes that want to see peace.

Come together,
Become one,
Peace isn't easy,
Unless you believe.

Help, stop,
Stop this happening,
You can help,
Help make the peace.
Hold hands,
Believe,
Put the guns down,
Hold fire,
Crash the bombs no more,
Together, the love will spread,
And make peace,
Peace on Earth!

Grace Winnie Brokenshire (13)
Ifield Community College, Crawley

MY PETS

Big, fat, fluffy
She is lovely
Grey, she is a cat.
Her name is Misty.

Small, skinny, fluffy
She is baby-like and lovely
Tabby, she is a cat.
Her name is Lilly.

Small, fat, fluffy
He is lovely
Grey, he is a rabbit.
His name is Thumper.

Last but not least
My rabbit Bugs
He is small, black and fluffy.
He is lovely.

I love my pets just as much as my family
But I can't choose just one.
My cat, Misty, is lovely but so is my rabbit, Thumper
My cat, Lilly, is shy but so is my rabbit, Bugs.
I love my pets just as much as I love all of you.

Chloe-Elise Milborrow (12)
Ifield Community College, Crawley

THE SKY IS . . .

When it's stormy
The sky is angry
When it's bright blue
It's happy
It's like the sea
Flying, it's like a blue whale
Surfing the clouds.

Josh Knight-Patto (11)
Ifield Community College, Crawley

MONSTER

I woke up and took a morning stroll,
I was ready to go, ready to roll.
Up and down the hills I went,
Round and round all the bends.

Suddenly, something scuttled,
I knew I was in trouble.
Then I heard a tear,
There was something there.

He had fierce, sharp teeth that matched his evil grin,
Big, yellow eyes looking hungrily at me.
He jammed me in his hand,
In his mouth, that's where I did land.

I went down the deep, dark hole.

I shouted and I screamed, 'Friends, friends!'
But I knew it was the end.

Then I heard a familiar voice.
'Oh, my friends, it's the boys!'
Bang! Crash!
Gurgle! Smash!

I went down the deep, dark hole.

Rebecca Beagles (11)
Ifield Community College, Crawley

LOOK UP HIGH

Look up high,
Up into the sky,
Where all you can see,
Are stars glistening,
In the moonlight,
Don't be shy,
Go on, just look up high.

Tia Djelassi (12)
Ifield Community College, Crawley

THE POETRY TRIALS - HAMPSHIRE & SUSSEX

THE LOVE WILL RUST

Tears run down her face
The pain really does hurt like
Memories she can't erase

Some people don't know how it feels
To have a broken heart
The grief is real

She should've been careful
She can't just trust
Because if you go too fast
The love will rust

She knew this would happen
He did it before
He's done it with everyone
And cut straight to the core

Acts all charming
That's where it starts
Then shoots her down
And breaks her heart

Because if you go too fast
The love runs out.

Chloe Rowland (11)
Ifield Community College, Crawley

UNTITLED

I saw a light.
It was so bright.
I had a fight.
I got knocked down.
I was on my way to Heaven.
I saw a strike.
It was another light
But they brought me back to life.

Jack Robinson (12)
Ifield Community College, Crawley

HEARTBREAK

There's no love for me
There's just pain
Why, why me?

I feel the pain
Every second of my life
There's no heart for me
And no love, *ever*.

Love is not the kind of thing
Everyone knows about
It's something big and important
You have to fight for it.

There are some good endings and bad endings
And sometimes it might never happen again
Just be positive of what you have
And make the best of it.

In my opinion
It's something you need
Just love each other
Nothing else but love.

Be happy and proud of what you have.

Wiktoria Wloszek (11)
Ifield Community College, Crawley

THE SKY

The sky is blue like a lagoon.
The sky is home to the fluffy clouds.
The sky is beautiful like a newborn baby with gentle, blue eyes.
The sky is as blue as a blue diamond.
The sky is a blanket that covers the Earth.
The sky is partnered with the candyfloss clouds.
The sky is God's best friend.
The sky can't compare to the beauty that is Mrs Thomas.

Jahmelya Muthen (11)
Ifield Community College, Crawley

DREAMS

I sleep at night with many thoughts
Good or bad, my care factor is nought
Even though nightmares haunt me
But happy dreams treat me

Is it worth it to make the roll
Running or loving in another world
Being stalked by a haunted doll
Or winning a pot of gold

Shall I really make the fall
Well at least it's better than a shopping mall

Going through portals every night
Then I start to see a light

Now I'm in the woods
Lost and bruised, hearing screams
A demon maybe, it could
I could not see as I'm blinded with leaves

Then I saw it
Then it bit
Later I wake up and think
Today I want to go to the ice rink.

Thebekshan Raguraj (11)
Ifield Community College, Crawley

LIGHT BEAMING DOWN

The light was beaming down on me,
As I stepped on the pitch
And placed the ball on the spot.
Everybody was cheering,
Then it went silent.
It was all down to me.
On this last penalty,
If I missed that would be it.

Ellis Robert Lawrence (12)
Ifield Community College, Crawley

ALONE IN THE SNOW

She froze. Still. In the snow.

Fear had struck her.
Thoughts rushing through her mind.
She was alone,
Alone in the snow.
In the middle of nowhere.
Nothing was in sight.
Nothing was in sight apart from the plain,
Pale, white snow
And a blonde-haired, blue-eyed girl.

She took a step forward.
Her foot sank and froze.
It became numb.
Then she heard a tap.

Something was growing and uncovering.
It was green with a red top.
A rose.
Now it was them.
Just them.
They were alone in the snow.

Katie Heuser (11)
Ifield Community College, Crawley

CUTE CATS!

Long, white whiskers,
Long, fluffy tail,
Leaving a trail of fur,
Night and day.

Lying down all day,
Until they find new prey.
Chasing it around,
Until it's pinned to the ground.

Piper Djelassi (12)
Ifield Community College, Crawley

THE SKY IS

The cloud's full of thoughts
And love bombs
Blow all
Over the place trying
To find a
Connection.
Planes whooshing in the
Gloomy night sky
The birds
Flap their wings as
They fly to
The end.
Insects trying to avoid
The giants as
They fly
And fly away past
The clouds to
The tomorrowland.

Lily-Pearl Kirby (12)
Ifield Community College, Crawley

LIGHT ...

She sat and waited for sunrise,
But nothing came,
She wiped the tears from her cheeks,
Then she saw the flame,
She edged closer to the door,
She knew she wasn't safe,
She rested against the windowpane,
Wondering if life would be the same,
It started to get lighter,
She asked herself if it was her to blame,
She said goodbye to her burning home,
She left and she was all alone.

Maisy Torrington (12)
Ifield Community College, Crawley

ENGLAND

Big red cross
Shiny white background
It's the flag of us

Shining armour
And expensive jewels
The Queen is our
Destiny.
We are so proud
Of our country and
Not used to not being
Proud.
Great Britain is us
The blue, white, red
All together make us
The greatest place on Earth
Be proud to come
And live here, we're kind, we're not blind.

Kayleigh Cumming (12)
Ifield Community College, Crawley

AUTUMN

Autumn leaves red, gold and brown
Falling, swirling and drifting down.
Prickly conkers cracking and popping,
Branches snap, acorns dropping.
Picking pumpkins, blackberries too,
Making a crumble for me and you.
Foggy mornings, frosty and cold,
A biting wind, blustery and bold.
Hibernating hedgehogs find somewhere to sleep,
You might get to see him if you don't make a peep.
The clocks go back and winter is near,
Christmas is coming, so it's time for some Christmas cheer.

Yasmine Apps (12)
Ifield Community College, Crawley

THE POEM ABOUT NOTHING!

I'm afraid I can't write poems,
I am not that good,
And when I try to write them,
They end up in a muddle.

So this poem is about nothing,
Nothing at all,
All it contains is nothing,
Nothing in the form of a poem.

Poems can be about anything,
This poem is about nothing.
Surely nothing is classed as something,
Although I may be wrong.

So if you can't write poems,
And if you aren't that good,
Next time you're stuck for ideas,
You can write about nothing!

Annie-Louise Thomas (12)
Ifield Community College, Crawley

THE SKY

The sky is a bright charm of hope
That brightens up the world.
The rainbow, the most beautiful thing in the world
With seven layers of colours.

The sky is blocks of steam
Blocking the gorgeous sunlight.
It is an endless daydream.

The sky is a festival of light
Dancing until dawn.
It is a mountain of clouds
Climbing higher every second
It protects our beautiful sky.

Michael Ellis (12)
Ifield Community College, Crawley

FALL

Summer draws its final breath
The winds begin to blow
Leaf by leaf each one will fall
Now the tree stands bare and tall

Summer draws its final breath
October's on its way
Children going trick or treating
Just like every year

Summer draws its final breath
The air is getting colder
Rainy days and cloudy skies
Are now taking over

Summer draws its final breath
The seasons are now changing
Summer's nearly gone
But autumn's in the making.

Migle Vasiliauskaite (12)
Ifield Community College, Crawley

THE MOON

The moon,
My night light,
It spills across my bedroom floor,
Shining light when bad times come,
The moon,
My night light,
My forever friend, forever outside my window,
For when I feel sad,
He lightens my mood,
The moon,
My night light,
Forever in my heart, forever right there.

Libby Bradbury (12)
Ifield Community College, Crawley

THE CORNER OF YOUR EYE

The corner of your eye,
A young girl stands still.
No motions but emotion,
In the corner of your eye.

The corner of your eye,
A forgotten stone engraved.
Lurking in the mysterious fog,
In the corner of your eye.

The corner of your eye,
The stain of tears left on her cheek.
A lost, tortured soul weeps and weeps,
In the corner of your eye.

The corner of your eye,
The memory locked away in your mind.
Counting the cost with someone you've lost,
In the corner of her eye.

Georgia Ryan (11)
Ifield Community College, Crawley

THE SKY

The sky is electric blue
The sun is bright, golden yellow
It is crashing and smashing
As lightning strikes below
Kaboom. The rustling of a whisper
And *tweet, tweet* go the birds.

The beautiful sunset of the sky
The flash and bang of a stormy night
Then the sun rises and is a fiery orange
Orange also is the vibration of the wind gasping for air
And *tweet, tweet* go the birds.

James Loader (11)
Ifield Community College, Crawley

FRIENDS!

Along the road you will see them
Old or new.
Along your life you will need them
Old or new.
Along their life they will break you.

They will be there in everyone's life,
Whether you need them or not.
Either way they need you.

You make each other complete.
You make each other perfect.
You make each other happy.

We all have them.
We all need them.
We all want them.

We would be nothing without them!

Tanya Shelby Megan Moore (12)
Ifield Community College, Crawley

ON THIS BATTLEFIELD

On the battlefield I hear the screams and cries.
I see the death and hardship of war.
I see the power of war and what it does to man from beginning to end.
We live, we die on the battlefield.

On this battlefield, lessons we have learnt will stay with us until the end
On this battlefield.

We fight as brothers through wind and rain,
The fire and the mud.

The misery of it all, things these men see,
They live, they die upon the battlefield.

Cameron Licence (14)
Ifield Community College, Crawley

THE SKY

The sky howls with pain as it wishes the pain to go away.
It has stormy nights and days to send the same to gain more again.
Its pink, orange and reds put summer to an end.
The night is the most important part of the day,
It leaves the sky to send tomorrow from today.
It smashes with its mighty grip although sometimes he may slip.
Well, the sunset is the best for me because it saves its oranges, purples and greens,
The leaves, oh how they gleam with the one thing below; that will be the tree,
The wind saws through the night and day to pressure the air and lay in the darkness for days,
I love the patterns in the sky, they can tell a person why. That person is me, who stood under the great, old oak tree,
So the clouds, wind and sky all want to wave you goodbye, have a great day and don't lie because the sky is determined to tell you why.

Maeve Hona Slocombe (11)
Ifield Community College, Crawley

STRANDED

Stranded, hanging there
Look up, I didn't dare.
Claws of my fate held high
Dangling there, mid sky.
Click and a zoom, we flew
The dragon within me withdrew.
Above the park
We sped as fast as a spark.
The track seemed to never end
Going round that final bend.
As furious as a tsunami tide
What a deadly ride.
Stranded, hanging there
Look down, I didn't dare.

Alice Giddings (12)
Ifield Community College, Crawley

THAT'S NOT WHAT MATTERS TO ME

You're always changing,
You're never the same,
In thunder, lightning and in rain,
You come in so many shapes and sizes,
But that's not what matters to me.

I don't know what to expect,
With you,
And your ever-changing appearance,
I don't judge you on such a thing as looks,
You may look scary,
But that's not what matters to me.

I couldn't care less about the way you look,
You could look like an ogre,
Or you could look like an angel,
But that's not what matters to me.

Chloe Madureira-Ward (12)
Ifield Community College, Crawley

LONDON'S GONE UP IN FLAMES

The church bells rang,
One hour of peace,
Emerging from the church,
The fire just over the bridge.

London is buzzing with terror and fear,
Babies screaming, children crying helplessly,
The screech of the sirens like a hyena's laugh.

As the smoke and flames engulf me,
I run and run,
No hope for the future,
My light, my hope all gone.

London's gone up in flames,
London's gone up in flames.

Hannah Flint
Ifield Community College, Crawley

THE STRANGE THING

Round the corner,
The bluebottles fly,
And there on the ground,
The strange thing lies,

The strange thing whistles, laughs and cries,
But you can never see its eyes,
And if you dare to go too close,
It'll be your life you miss the most,

The clothes it wears are soot black,
He has arthritis,
And a hunched back,

The legend has it,
Someone's seen his face,
But who is he, is he near this place?

Morgan Rose Sladovich (11)
Ifield Community College, Crawley

THE SKY

The sky is an oasis of calm
Where bird songs sound like
They are being played on harps.
The rustle of leaves through the breeze
Like the whistle of a flute.

Sounds of stormy skies
Crash and bang
Horrendous thunder is all that seeps through your ear canal
Apart from the zap of lightning that,
Just like itself, makes your eyes flicker.

The most beautiful moment of the sky though
Is when the orange sun
Soft and mellow as it could be
Softly sinks under her fiery, yellow horizon.

Joshua Ansfield (11)
Ifield Community College, Crawley

STARS AND STARS

My mum always told me,
Grandad's up there,
Stars shined,
As if he heard me,
A beam of light shot across the sky,
Mum said make a wish,
I made a wish, I knew it wouldn't come true,
The moon shone,
A flash of light spread across the sky,
I could hear him,
Always believe,
No one wants to see their light go out,
But my grandad's did.
Stars and stars are everywhere.

Caitlin Hollis (12)
Ifield Community College, Crawley

THE SUN

The sun is bright,
Like a very bright light,
The sun rose upon us,
On a day that I like,
The light is dimmer,
As dim as can be,
The light shining,
Like it's on TV!
It was bright time,
Light time,
But now it is night-time,
Night-time,
Night-time,
The light is now the moonlight.

Mason Jones (12)
Ifield Community College, Crawley

THE CAVE

The anger grew inside me
The sadness soaked my heart
I knew I had to face it
I knew the face in the cave would come

It would come forward
Until it couldn't come any closer
This can't continue
I knew I had to face it someday
Whatever it was.

I can do this
I can, can't I?
No, I can't do it
The face in the cave is coming.

Poppy Honey Wright (11)
Ifield Community College, Crawley

THE FOX

The fox pads through the snow, not knowing where to go.
His mother's encouraging howls were distant and lost in the windy night.
The fox let out his own squeak, only a whisper.
Trees turned into shadows, shadows turned into faces,
Faces turned into people with razor-sharp claws and teeth.
He kept walking through the cloudy mist, though the whispers called him to turn back ...
Snow crunched beneath the little fox's feet and tiny snowflakes covered his rusty fur, making him shiver.
Seconds turned into minutes, minutes turned to hours, hours turned into days and he found his mother.
Only it was just like Bambi.

Grace Owen (11)
Ifield Community College, Crawley

SHINE BRIGHT

The only one that shines,
Is mine,
Be with me every step of the way,
Every day,
You're mine,
I will never give up,
Even if I'm away,
I will always be by your side,
In my mind,
In my thoughts,
No matter what,
You're mine,
Shine bright like you have never before.

Sophie Davis-Lyons (13)
Ifield Community College, Crawley

LIGHT

The light that guides you through the unknown
The light that reveals any dark corners
The light that is there for you
The light that you can rely on, the light that watches you
The light that helps you
The light that is your friend
The light that you shine when you smile
The light that never abandons you
Disappears when you need it most and leaves you blind,
Lost, helpless, cold, forgotten, silent blackness of the dark
Which dominates all around you until everything's gone.
So, never lose hope and faith in light,
Because if you stay with light, it stays with you.

Abdul Sidhom (12)
Ifield Community College, Crawley

THE SKY

The sky is a place of peace and relaxation
The sky is a home for the clouds
The sky is a place we dream about
Warm
Bright
Paradise
The sky is your mood: cloudy, sad; sunny, happy
The sky is your emotions: rain, tears; thunder, anger
The sky is the place we dream about
Warm
Bright
Paradise
The endless, blue blanket.

Morgan Scanlon Snell (11)
Ifield Community College, Crawley

SKY

The fiery, orange sky is a yellowish gold
Burnt to a gooey, lemon feel,
Mixed with a stunning red rose dye
To give it that lovely touch
And to make the flaming gold sun stand out
Over the tall, green hills.
The daisies stand like white, fluffy pillows
On a green stem,
With a yellow bee harvesting pollen
To make gooey, yummy honey
To eat with freshly baked bread.

Toby Russell O'Reilly (11)
Ifield Community College, Crawley

SKY POEM

The sky is a heaven of blue
The sky is filled with calm birds chirping
The sky can be a haze of rain
The sky can be lakes of fog
The sky has scattered powder-puff clouds
The sky is a blanket of darkness
The sky is a shock of lightning
The sky is as dark as ink
The sky has a one find morning
And the sky is what you see every calm day.

Andre Dos Santos (11)
Ifield Community College, Crawley

FRIENDSHIP WAVES

Friends are like waves,
There are highs and lows,
A calm and a storm,
Crashes and bangs,
They can damage you,
But never break you,
You can be drowned in love and happiness,
Or drowned in a mixture of sadness,
But whatever happens they will carry you out of harm,
And sail you into happiness.

Tilly Leigh Fewtrell (12)
Ifield Community College, Crawley

DIFFERENT LIGHTS

Gaze up high
Look up into the sky
Admire the different lights

Stars dance around
The glowing light
The sun and the moon's
Beautiful light shines
Upon our land

Do you like the different lights?

Habibah Ahmed (12)
Ifield Community College, Crawley

THE MOONLIGHT

Moonlight shines over the sea
It glistens like the sun on a warm summer's day
As I watch it, I see it glow

In the night it's like a sudden show
If you follow it
It may lead you somewhere
But you've got to believe me
The moonlight
My night light.

Megan Boswell (13)
Ifield Community College, Crawley

THE DARKNESS

Lost inside the darkness of my mind
Ignorant, impossible and impatient people
Going out of their way to be mean
How can this be
To find the light you must find your soul.

Kai Dwyer (12)
Ifield Community College, Crawley

SMOKE

The killer of all, he can make you cry without words.
He can make the world disappear before your eyes.
He is involved in all wars, the blinder of all eyes.
Make a runner before he gets to you, before you know it he will eat you too.
He comes into your lungs, eats them from inside, then he leaves them to rot for years and years.
You are a target waiting to be fired at, watch your back before *smoke attacks!*

Mohammed Rahman (11)
Ifield Community College, Crawley

LIGHT POEM

Moonlight, moonlight, shine bright like a light
Every time I look at the moon I am always right
Every time I look at the stars they are bright
The moon is always white
This is the time
Now look at the sky, it is night.

Joel Peacock (11)
Ifield Community College, Crawley

THE SKY

The sky is as dark as the depths of the ocean
But infinitely more deep.
The sky is a fiery blaze at sunset.
The sky at night is the darkness prowling around.
The sky is as blue as the Great Barrier Reef.
The sky is an enormous blanket of blue.

Charlie Marshall Miller (11)
Ifield Community College, Crawley

THE SKY

The sky is wonderful
With a touch of sunlight and sunshine.
At night-time the sky is vibrant
Fiery like a devil's house.
The sky is sometimes cloudy and stormy
But it's like lightning coming out of Zeus' staff.

Nabil Mehmood (11)
Ifield Community College, Crawley

CATS

Walking around, not knowing what to do,
Sleeping all day, not having a clue,
Purring for food, night and day,
In the middle of the floor, that's where she lays.

Leaving trails of fur everywhere she goes,
Big, long, white whiskers near her nose,
Long, brown tail follows her behind,
Wags it side to side using her mind.

Amelie Kenvin (12)
Ifield Community College, Crawley

MUM

Mum is such a
Special word,
The loveliest
I've ever heard.

You are better by far
Than all the rest.
These four words say it
'Mum, you're the best.'

Nitharshika Gnanachandran (11)
Ifield Community College, Crawley

THE SKY IS ...

Baby blue love
Where dreams come true
White, nice clouds
A bird's home
A place of happiness
A place of thoughts
Black, mean clouds
Love and laughter.

Nieve Jorgensen Smallwood (11)
Ifield Community College, Crawley

THIS IS THE LOVE

Romeo is the sun and
Juliet is the moon,
One works at day and
Another one works at night
And when it's afternoon
They kiss and go back to work.
This is their love.

Ricardo Lima Castaneda (12)
Ifield Community College, Crawley

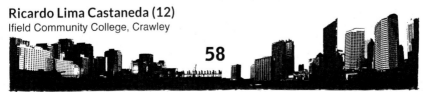

THE PINK TRUTH!

Trapped in two corners,
Forced into one,
Drowned by the pressures,
The waves have won.
I hide from the pink truth
Underneath the ocean,
Hiding from reality,
Ignoring the news
And the firing of guns.
Stereotypes justify my lies,
My truths sent away across the shore,
Arriving in another country.
I'm trapped in two corners,
Forced into one.
Don't know who to choose,
The waves or my own sun?
Or should I hide inside the ocean?

Harrison Coughlan (13)
King's School, Brighton

DARK, BLACK ... SPACE

Darkness. The blackness of space.
It fills me with empty sorrows.
The world I once knew to be so enormous,
I can now fit in the palm of my hands.
The sea is deep blue and the land emerald-green.
Loneliness gradually fills me.
I am alone and isolated for all eternity.
The distant stars twinkle above me,
Sparkling in the dark night sky.
The wind never whistles
And the rain never falls
For I am in dark, black space for all eternity.

Aiden Perrin (13)
King's School, Brighton

HALF A HEART

The moment you left this world, my heart split in two,
One went black and curdled, and the other died with you.
I lie in bed at night, filled with pain and heartbreak,
I curl up on the floor, my head in my hands.

I think of you every day, but it just fills me with pain,
I scream!
I'm not ready to face the truth, you're gone and not coming back.

I wish I could re-live the good times we had,
I wish I could appreciated your little quirks,
But now you're gone . . . please come back.

I feel mad at you, I feel you don't care,
You put me through so much pain,
Yet I still forgive you.

I went to the doctors today, my mum took me.
He said I've got depression,
That's how you make me feel.

I wish I could see you just one more time,
Just to say our last goodbye,
But until it's my turn to go,
I have to live with half a heart.

Charlotte Wills (13)
King's School, Brighton

FADING LIGHT

Hopelessness, dread and torture
They all come for me
My heart frozen, feeling numb
Seeking the burning flame, that isn't lasting.

Fury, temper and trouble,
Once friends of mine,
My eyes bewildered, my thoughts sealed
On the edge of insanity, a small step it shall seem.

Distress, idiocy and depression
Just won't go beyond me
My memories faultless, my future in doubt
Purpose hidden in shadows.

Distrust, slavery and misery
Have once more come,
My heart is cast away, my love fallen
I have done bad things and I have become them.

Love, peace and courage
The light inside me fades away
Darkness seeks its opportunity
You see freedom has a way of destroying things.

Skye Leonie Collacott Williamson (13)
King's School, Brighton

WORLD AT WAR

A long time ago, the world was at peace
No one was treated differently
War was not necessary, we were one
We all wish that this was still the case
Time moves on, so do we
People change, minds shaped
Ideas of right and wrong change the nation
To this day, there is war and pain
People dying of murder and starvation
Yet we still have to believe we were once in union
Today's world is not compatible with God's design!

Xenia Howard (13)
King's School, Brighton

MISSING

A boy
Sprung against a snow
His hands stung from morning glow
His arms around his only sack
Frost composing on his back
And though his nails hung on string
In his bag was post to bring
For rich and poor, for old and young
Though morning air would stab his lung
A boy
Sat in icy lair
Lips rang on bony stair
Midnight sky with cloud so low
A boy
Of all a month of snow.

Annabell Claire Agate (15)
Oriel High School, Crawley

THE POETRY TRIALS - HAMPSHIRE & SUSSEX

SPEED

Zooming through the street,
Defeating thousands of deadly feats,
Dodging, weaving, undefeated,
Zipping, whizzing, never repeated
By any passer-by.
Look straight at me and you'll fly,
Shooting, soaring through the sky
Or on the road, on a bike,
Just a blur you will like
The joyous breeze
Left by me.

Jacob Stephen Cooper (14)
Oriel High School, Crawley

PEACE AFTER LIFE

There is a will for my heart left to go, scattered over fields
And under the white snow.
And the hearts that have been broken will once again be heard,
As they live another life, on another Earth.

Summertime the grass grows high
Clouds swiftly moving in the sky,
To open the sun to make flowers grow,
As all that was lost will once again flow.

In the night deep within light, shaded by the trees,
Hear the sound of rushing water and the gentle breeze.
Trying to touch the people that we love,
As someone's looking down at us above.

I hope that love will come again and find our souls at rest,
There, life will come to us, at its very best.
But life will come and go, that we all must know.
And the souls that live together, will dance again forever.

Jazzmyn Ella Young (11)
Ratton School, Eastbourne

THE RIDDLE OF YOU

Awash with anxiety
Ridden with hate
For the birds and the bees
From a faraway place

A land of mysteries
Too tall to be true
Filled with riddles
In all different hues

Love me or hate me
I am what you seek
Take a walk through
Go on, take a peek

I am all your nightmares
Your wishes come true
I live under your bed
Or deep within you

And now you are pondering
Looking for the truth
But can't you see?
Look within!
I am you, only you.

Aisling Nevill (14)
Ratton School, Eastbourne

IT DOESN'T MATTER

I said my fish died,
My mum said,
'Don't worry, it doesn't matter,
We'll get a new one.'

I said the skies are cloudy,
My friend said,
'Don't worry, it doesn't matter,
Water poured from the skies.'

I said my nan was in hospital,
My teacher said,
'Don't worry, it doesn't matter,
You can still do PE.'

I was absent for three days,
My nan died.

I went back to school,
My first lesson was PE.
My teacher said,
'Don't worry, you'll be fine.'
It didn't mean I was.

After all, it doesn't matter.

Abbie Lauren Windham (15)
Ratton School, Eastbourne

A SYMPHONY FOR THE FALLEN

Choirboys will fall in line
From church bells to the muster
Prayers from preachers
Sons of teachers
When choirboys come marching

They go away with so much hope
And come back home from hell
From symphony
To infantry
When choirboys come marching

As shells explode and muskets blow
They carry on and on
Their voices ache
Their bodies break
When choirboys come marching

They hear the final call and march
Until the break of day
The bugle blows
And down they go
When choirboys stop marching

Jake Worrell (15)
Ratton School, Eastbourne

THE POETRY TRIALS - HAMPSHIRE & SUSSEX

LOVE AND HATE . . .

Those two words, true love, that strong word, hate.
Both equally powerful, hurtful and meaningful.
The little love poems and secret admirers,
The pranks and plans of revenge.
The world is full of hatred, full of emotions,
Full of decisions and heartbreak.
Is there such a thing as a happy ending in the dark world we call
home,
This harsh reality we're forced to live?
Is there such a thing as love at first sight, or heaven or hell?
All these questions we ask ourselves every day, every night, all our
lives.
Love and hate . . .
The Valentine's Day cards and gifts.
The Halloween tricks and scares.
The crushes we have.
Those answers we want, like does he hate me, does he love me?
Does she hate me, does she like me?
Everyone, young and old, faces these questions in life.
It's all simply love and hate.
Love and hate . . .

Amy Bleach (12)
Ratton School, Eastbourne

COMPUTERS

C ompiled work and homework
O ther devices are touchscreen
M emory sticks are for doing work anywhere
P rinters are good for printing work
U SB slots are good for putting in a mouse
T ablets are used in schools
E verything is possible
R AM stands for Random Access Memory
S peakers are good for listening to loud music.

Freddie George Cullen (11)
Ratton School, Eastbourne

THE MIRRORS THAT ARE US

We hide and we love
We cry and we laugh
I smile, you smile
You cry, I cry
It's strange how we are all so similar yet so different
We see black, we see white
We see animals, we see life
I see you but I see someone awesome
It's funny how love works
It is the reason why we see as we do
Seeing someone you love is seeing
Joy, sadness, a true wonder
It's what makes you think
What if we are all mirrors
But we only have one reflection
And it's our reflection we love?

Kia Howell (14)
Ratton School, Eastbourne

ANIMOSITY

Vicious revenge, bitter pain,
Ingrained forever on a decaying brain.
Metal against metal, fire against fire
A poisonous secret, that shall never transpire.
Engulfed in hate, eyes pure animosity,
Blinded by rage, too much to see.

Now pale heart, porcelain pieces,
An undying need for revenge, it never ceases.
Heart enveloped in loathing, a sweet, revengeful vine.
Quite a sadistic pleasure, a dark soul ready to entwine.
A plunging trench of retaliation.
A scary way of getting elation.

Lynette Riley (12)
Ratton School, Eastbourne

SCHOOL

S even o'clock, I wake up to an annoying sound
C limbing out of bed, I hear Mum call, 'Breakfast!'
H urrying downstairs like a hurricane, I realise it's school
O h, it's time to go to that place called school!
O w, ow, it hurts (let's try the old skiving), I can't go
L ook, I hate school and don't want to go, is that a crime?

T ime to go in! The bell said *ding-dong*, I wont, you will never
take me alive!
I 'm in. Tutor time is a-go, I roll in James Bond style
M aggie, get off the floor and sit down, *now!*
E nd of school, I run out the door shouting 'School's out for
summer!' My tutor comes shouting, 'It's time for period 1.' *No!*

Maggie Rayner (11)
Ratton School, Eastbourne

PARKOUR ESCAPE

Running over and scaling walls,
Trying to escape, trying so hard to cross the landscape.
Over the hills and through the trees,
They are always pursuing.
The government's fees are going up
To the hunters they hire
And I am a wanted man I see.
Trying to escape with a suitable plan.
Sleeping rough so as not to be found.
One night on the border, I hear gunshots coming my way.
They know I am here, time to scurry away.
I made it. I really tried.
I'm home now and safe.
I will never be chased across the landscape.

Dominic Bakker (13)
St George Catholic College, Southampton

MIDNIGHT HUNTER

The white-bellied hunter with shining pearl teeth
Glides through the moonlit sea.
Like a speeding torpedo, a monster released
She has her whole life to be free.

The water is cloudy and inky, dark black,
They feel her presence here.
Not Arctic, nor reef, not shallow but deep,
The sea's anything but clear.

Midnight is best for the hunt to begin,
It's when most prey is unaware . . .
Her beady, black eye flicks from right to left,
But still giving nothing her stare.

A faraway shape she spies on the surface
Her dagger-like body she swerves,
Curious what this new object might be,
And hoping that dinner is served.

Larger and larger the shadow still grows,
As she rises from undersea depths,
But just as she finds out what this shape might be . . .

The hunter is caught in a net.

Thrashing and crashing, she tries to break free,
But the fisherman's net is too strong.
Once, the most terrible ocean nightmare,
Now trapped, knowing death won't be long.

Captured, defeated and truly destroyed,
She longs for her ocean domain.
She thinks of the days chasing fur seals for food,
Now lying in absolute shame.

Remembering in gloom her predator days,
She thinks of her razor-sharp teeth
And a plan to free her from fishermen's hands,
To continue her life beneath.

THE POETRY TRIALS - HAMPSHIRE & SUSSEX

She slices and dices the net with her teeth,
With the urge to be free still inside.
With one final bite, the victim is free
And into the blue she glides.

The trawler is gone and the dawn starts to break,
The hunter's now free to attack.
Forever she shall be most utterly feared
And never to ever look back.

Anthony Baillie-Powell (13)
St George Catholic College, Southampton

WHAT AM I?

What am I?
I'll follow if you lead
I'll lead if you follow
I'll help if you need
I'll protect you also

I'll sing if you dance
I'll write the song
I'll join in if you ask
It doesn't matter if it goes wrong

I'll support you when you play
No matter what you do
I'll give you presents on your birthday
I'm always there for you.

Alec Mills (13)
St George Catholic College, Southampton

FOOTBALL IS FUN

F antastic ways of playing
O pponent will do their best to win
O wn goals can happen in matches
T all people are useful to header the ball
B est players try to show off
A ll players can play fair in the game
L earn new ways to play
L ots of players argue with the referee

G enius people are good at games
A ll players show respect to each other
M any people are not good at games
E vents happen when people are not interested.

Jeswin Kallukaran (12)
St George Catholic College, Southampton

UNTITLED

When the final bell rings on a Friday afternoon,
Everyone rushing, wanting to get home soon.
Approaching the house, the TV welcoming me in.
Putting my bag down, I sit on the floor.
Grasping the controller, powering her on.
The emotions right inside me fill the whole room up.
All the negative things in my mind pushed aside.
Only one thing on my mind
And that is the soothing beep sound when it's on.
I put in the disc, the main menu opens up.
The rest is up to you.

Kenneth Cacacho (13)
St George Catholic College, Southampton

THE POETRY TRIALS - HAMPSHIRE & SUSSEX

FLICK OF DA WRIST

Look at the flick of the wrist,
The swish of the net,
The feel of the wind,
These are my favourite things.
The jump to overcome your enemy,
The sound of your trainers screeching on the floor.
The ball is in your hands, now sprint to the hoop . . .
But don't look back.
A few cross-overs here and there,
Under the leg, through their defence.
He shoots . . . he scores.

Ben Patrucco (13)
St George Catholic College, Southampton

FAITHFUL FRIENDSHIPS

Friendships are the most vital part,
Like the beautiful sound of a strumming harp,
The sun rose up, the sunset down,
And here I am, with the two-faced clowns,
They abuse me, repeatedly call me names,
My anger is roaring, like a scolding flame.

At the end of the day, pain is yet to wash away,
Sunset is near, my mind cannot clear,
But before I sleep, into the deepest sleep,
I forgive my betrayers, though I still weep.

Matthew Wilson Levy (13)
St George Catholic College, Southampton

IMAGINATION IS ...

Imagination is ...
Finding a gold mine in your room,
Finding a pot of gold at the end of a rainbow,
Finding a magic ring that tells your mood,
Making a new friend that's an elephant,
Making a 'best tasting' stew,
Making Dad the pirate king,
Bringing the car into the house,
Bringing a stick of awesomeness back home,
Bringing a mud pie in and eating it.

Patrick James Goodwin (12)
St George Catholic College, Southampton

COMPUTER

C all it whatever you want
O verall, great to play games
M ultiplayer is the best
P lay games all you want
U pgrade it, make it better
T alk to all your friends
E veryone needs one
R PGs are the best.

Joshua Corry (13)
St George Catholic College, Southampton

THE POETRY TRIALS - HAMPSHIRE & SUSSEX

CRICKET

C ool game
R eally fun
I like to play
C hallenging
K eep calm
E xtra quick and fit you must be
T he rules are simple.

Ranjit Landa (12)
St George Catholic College, Southampton

SELFISH

Selfish he is
My husband I mean
Haven't seen a penny in months
Greed runs through him like blood runs through veins
'We can share it, my love,' he said
Lying through his teeth
Under his silk sheets
Half my earnings I share with that pig!

It doesn't matter anymore
He will be dead by four
Lying on the ground
Under his bedsheet mound
His throat will be slit
Nobody will know . . .

It was his wife who did it

I will watch his thick blood pour
Onto the oak wood floor
In our bedroom he will lay
I will wait one more day
All the money will be mine
And that selfish pig will die.

Katherine White (14)
St Paul's RC College, Burgess Hill

BIRDS

I sit there, the warm grass tickling my feet,
An old, hard stump as my seat.
Then a shadow cast over me,
All those birds in the air, so weightless and free.

From where I am standing,
I can see beautiful birds landing,
On the cold, hard railings scattered around Brighton pier.

As they swoop and dive,
The sensation makes me feel alive.
All those birds in the air,
I just find it so unfair.

The Brighton beach all pebbled and hard,
The only person, a single lifeguard.
Then birds so glorious to just watch and see,
Those birds in the air flying over me!

As I stand alone looking for a friend,
A bird comes down and sits near the bend.
It looks up at me as if to say,
'I've been your friend day after day.'

Then he flew off with one single tweet.
Goodbye, old friend, until next time we meet.

Kate Veronica Brown (11)
St Paul's RC College, Burgess Hill

I AM NOT ALONE

Twisted trees look at me
With their scowling faces,
The brittle branches break beneath me
With a sharp snap.
The damp, soggy marsh covers my feet.
I am not alone.

I stumble across a foreboding, pointed
Gable house,
Its boarded up with smashed windows,
'Keep Out' signs all around,
Shadows looming in the distance,
Eerie sounds echo through the twisted trees.
I am not alone.

Faces looming through the windows
As if someone is there,
Crows cast shadows through the murky water.
I edge closer to the house,
The musty smell of rotting wood,
Footprints fresh in the ground,
I am not alone.

I feel something touch me,
The brush of a hand.
I turn to face my destiny;
Do you think I'm alone?

Sam Bouckaert (13)
St Paul's RC College, Burgess Hill

MY LIFE AS SCISSORS

The zip moved and light flooded in!
I'd been lying in that case for days.
Nobody to talk to,
Nobody to joke with.

Finally, he picked me up,
I loved the feeling of warm hands
Touching my handles,
But I knew what that meant.
It only meant one thing.
Murder!

As he slid the paper out of the drawer,
I was dreading the thought of
Cutting through his innocent body,
You could tell that the paper was dreading it too.

As my jaws opened
And bit into the sheet,
I could hear the paper shouting;
'How could you?'
'Help!'
'Ooww!'
I did not want to do this,
But I had to.
I was forced to!

Once I was done killing my dear friend,
I felt dreadful.
Sometimes I really wish
I could be something else;
A pencil,
A rubber, *anything!*
Being scissors, is obviously
Not something for me.

Helena Walasek (12)
St Paul's RC College, Burgess Hill

THE FIGURE

The invasive, insidious vines
Crept up the castle wall and
As I approached the scarred, broken door,
I felt the strong wind,
Daring to kick me into the abyss below.

Flashes of lightning threatened
To strike the castle, which was
Teetering on the edge of the cliff,
Tortured roots trying to escape
From the rocky outcrop
Into the murky sea.

A dark, malevolent figure
Appeared at the window
In a flash of lightning,
White holes staring at me
Where there should be eyes,
Slowly destroying my soul.

Icy hail, like daggers,
Slashed at me, trying
To rip my flesh.
I knocked on the hollow,
Foreboding doors,
Then in a flash,
The figure was behind me.
It came at me
And suddenly everything went dark
And I heard a crunch.

Sam Johnson (13)
St Paul's RC College, Burgess Hill

I AM NOT ALONE

A sudden flash of lightning lights the sky,
The trees sway as the abrupt wind comes rushing by,
Dead silent, not a sound could I hear.

I am isolated,
I can't escape from here.
I stumble to an abandoned house,
Unloved and lonely,
Staring through the broken windows,
My dark and worried eyes,
A shiver travelling turbulently
Through my spine.

Another step?
On the crunching leaves,
The foreboding gargoyles stare at me,
Through their dark, malevolent eyes,
Judging my every move as I walk by.

I am not alone, the foreboding fog circles me,
The wind starts whistling,
The ice-cold rain pours down aggressively.
The abandoned house crumbles away,
I start to run far away,
Pushing the winding fog,
But something's stopping me from leaving.
I have to stay.

Catty Broz (13)
St Paul's RC College, Burgess Hill

I'LL SEE CHRISTMAS AGAIN . . .

They came running out of the smoke
Panic set in their eyes
Coughing, desperate, soon they would choke
Gas! Quick!
We reached for our masks, nervous and fumbling
But someone's too late, they're blind and stumbling
Then in the distance we hear a roar
The Germans are advancing
At the crack of dawn.
Guns blaze
People fall
Anyway, what is the point of it all?
Then the shells drop
We know something is wrong
We try to fight back
But they're too many, too strong
Tanks come first
Our trenches are useless
Then come the bullets in short little bursts
A pain in my leg
My thigh feels wet
I fall to the ground as the stampede comes on
I hope I'll get to see Christmas again
It's only tomorrow
Surely I can survive that long . . .

Thomas O'Connor (11)
St Paul's RC College, Burgess Hill

TRUE LOVE

The sun only shines, when you are in my view
For I can only love you.
My heart only beats just for you,
For I would run a hundred miles to be there for you
Whenever you need me, for I love you.
When you walk outside the birds tweet
And the flowers sprout.
When I'm all alone, you will never leave my mind,
For every moment you're by my side
I treasure so deeply, it's hard to forget every minute of it.
When I look at you I think, do I really deserve you?
For you are so beautiful, my heart aches for you.
I wake up in the morning and the first thing I see is you.
It makes my day, then I think I can never let you go.
When I look up at the night sky,
I look at the brightest star and it reminds me of you
Because I love you and only you.
When I'm all alone on the deepest, darkest days,
You come along with a smile on your face
And make the darkness run away.
For when hope is nearly lost, you appear and hope rises
And all is not lost.
I have written this just for you because I love you.

Josh Mustafa (13)
St Paul's RC College, Burgess Hill

BLANK

Blank is a bouncing start, a natural birth
It is a tranquil of a vacant room in which you stay
It's a bird, light and bright, flying on its own
But it is also withdrawn and tastes of marshmallows
It has a touch of books
Jack Frost sprinkling diamonds on a floor
A touch of cotton wool and fur.

Erin Griffin (12)
St Paul's RC College, Burgess Hill

THE POETRY TRIALS - HAMPSHIRE & SUSSEX

WINTERLAND

Snowflakes on your eyelashes
Birds on the trees
Wind in your face
It's like it was meant for you

Presents under the tree
Logs on the fire
Gingerbread for you and me

Snowmen and snowball fights
Carolers out in the streets
Mistletoe above the door
Stockings by your bed
Can't wait to open them in the morning

Santa's bells
And magic reindeer
Can hear them at night
Cosy in bed

Today's the day
We have a roast and play
All the games we got from Santa

I love Christmas.

Kaitlin Teresa Grace Griffin (13)
St Paul's RC College, Burgess Hill

DARK AND GLOOMY WOODS

As I approach the dark and gloomy woods
I began to wonder whether I should
The daunting trees tower over me
Autumn leaves scattered like debris
The branches crunch beneath my feet
The birds, once happy, no longer tweet
Something lurks at the end of the tree
But its shadow's not people that I see.

Callum Smith (13)
St Paul's RC College, Burgess Hill

MY COW

My cow got out of the field one day
He climbed in my car and drove away
I jumped on my bike and followed him so
Treading through the crystal, crunchy snow

I saw him in a shop drinking coffee
So I spied on him, eating Banoffee

Next, to the toy shop he went
And picked up a toy cow
I need to get to the bottom of this and now

The next place he went really puzzled me
It was to the farm down the lane next to the old oak tree
He looked at the other cows in their herd
And overhead flew a bird
She said, 'Come on, look around the bend
All he's ever needed is a friend'

The next morning when my cow was home
He opened his eyes and was not alone
For there in front of him was a friend

I hope you liked it, the end.

Ella Rose Peck (12)
St Paul's RC College, Burgess Hill

THE POETRY TRIALS - HAMPSHIRE & SUSSEX

THE GRAVEYARD

That's it! *Snap!* My mood has changed.
It's her fault, how could she? She must be deranged.
An accident? No, there's no excuse for this act.
She killed him, my love and that is a fact!
Revenge is a dish best served cold.
A murder investigation, it will all unfold.

Give her some medicine, all she'll see is a blur,
Or a drop of poison in food only for her.
No! Something different, not enough pain,
Not enough of a story, not enough of a gain.
Maybe a gun or a pistol, a shot to each leg?
Wait a few minutes before the bullet's in the head.
Good idea, just a bit too loud...
A knife in the back, make her scream and shout.

Where? When? The graveyard at night.
I'll creep up from behind her, give her a gasping fright.
Deep into winter, wind, rain and snow;
The frightful story will end in great woe.
Finally, it's finished, my devious plan.
Her foolishness has cost her her life to my bloody hands.

Guy Batt (13)
St Paul's RC College, Burgess Hill

TAKE ME AWAY

This place taunts me,
Every time the bell chimes,
My nose sizzles from the stench,
My hands shake from the terror,
My lips are as dry as a hot summer's day

I am trapped
Trapped in this place,
Trapped in the place I created years ago

As the fog burns my eyes,
I fight the air in front of me,
Gasping for something, anything

Then darkness,
All I see is darkness,
The nothingness is enough to scare a monster,
With big, shiny, red eyes and green slime
Dripping off its mouldy skin

Take me away!

Alexandra Baker (14)
St Paul's RC College, Burgess Hill

A MAN IN WHITE

In the dark
Of the blackest night,
A man in white roams the road,
A vial of poison in his pocket,
A lock of hair in his locket.
A vendetta of love,
Ghosts of pasts haunt the memories,
The poison swirls and boils,
Ready for its next victim,
Waiting angrily with its blood-red glow.

Connor Tavener (13)
St Paul's RC College, Burgess Hill

THE NIGHT

In the dark of night,
Some thunder strikes,
I hear a scream
And it comes from the graveyard.
I am intrigued but at the same time anxious.
I walk through a gate
And past a lake.
I hear footsteps
And get scared.
The fog is blinding,
But suddenly I hear another scream.
This time it sounded much closer
Within touching distance.
I then see a flash
And hear a bang.
This was a mistake,
But it's too late now.

Ben Saunders (13)
St Paul's RC College, Burgess Hill

DOG

Dog, why are you so silly, oh?
With your floppy ears and your wet nose,
You wag your tail in the sunshine,
Asleep in my conservatory,
You can't find a ball even if it's right under your nose,
Or a stick in a bush that has been thrown,
You wolf down your food like you have never been fed before,
And then you come back and beg for more.
You chase cats and snap at flies,
You fight with your brother and you smell,
You jump in ponds and roll in mud,
You woof at things and dry yourself on the sofa,
But I love you, Dog.

Ethan Sumner (12)
St Paul's RC College, Burgess Hill

BOB THE BLOB

Meet Bob. Bob is a blob.
Bob and I have been friends forever.
When me and Bob go to the coffee shop
He gets the ploppy latte.
Me and Bob laugh a lot.
Once Bob went missing one day.
He hopped on a bus and it drove away
I ran after the bus, screaming and shouting, 'No, no, no!'
Bob was my best friend
While I was running, I saw Bob out the window.
I waved at him, then he looked rather puzzled.
Bob the blob turned away, jumped out the bus
And ran my way.
Bob gave me one of his huge hugs.
I love Bob, I care for Bob, we have so much fun!
Bob is not only a blob, he is my friend.
I'm with Bob till the end.

Macy Phillips (13)
St Paul's RC College, Burgess Hill

MY WW1 KENNINGS POEM

Soldiers shooting,
Bombs exploding,
Countries colliding,
Guns firing,
Fingers shaking.

Officers ordering,
Trenches trembling,
Men dying,
Rats scattering,
Armies crumbling.

Poppies remembering...

Henry Tomkins (11)
St Paul's RC College, Burgess Hill

THE POETRY TRIALS - HAMPSHIRE & SUSSEX

SHADOWS

Shadows, yet nobody is around me,
Cries of loneliness, but there is nobody there.
The trees seem to be screaming out to me
In the silence of the night.
A drop of cold rain trickled down the back of my neck
And ran slowly down my spine.
It made me shiver,
Alone but I felt a presence of another.
I heard a deafening scream.
I turned around.
Upon the hill stood an unearthly shadow.
Its eyes were filled with loneliness but yet it seemed to be seeking
revenge.
It glided supernaturally through the air towards me.
I wanted to run,
I wouldn't move. Was it all over?

Niamh Bridger (13)
St Paul's RC College, Burgess Hill

BLANK

Blank is a raw vision, a crystal mist to a plain day
Blank is a calm light, a plain wall in front of you
Blank is a crisp quilt, a folio of futuristic journals
Blank is a passion, a prior passion
Blank is a word, a colossal word, a spry word
Blank is a margin, a margin for opportunity
Blank is a crack, a gap to stow away in
Blank is a plain pathway, a way to build your coming gasp
Blank is a way, a way to mouth your opinion
Blank is a chronology, a raw addition to your past
Blank is a birth, a start to a long duration
Blank is urbanity, a way to occur with no action
Blank is a canvas, a capacity waiting for paint
Blank is a raw vision, a crystal mist to a plain day.

Lucy Amerio (12)
St Paul's RC College, Burgess Hill

I'M NOT ALONE

I'm not alone,
Someone or something is out there,
Their beady eyes stalk my dreams,
A cold, bare hand dragged along my neck.

I'm not alone.

They watch my every move,
They're planning an attack on me,
I don't know when or why,
But then I feel a presence.
I see a shadow,
Holding something deadly.
Do I scream? Do I shout?
No one is here to save me,
I gasp as a weapon comes closer . . .

I was not alone.

Niamh Gallagher (13)
St Paul's RC College, Burgess Hill

HAUNTED

The house was dark, cold and dingy.
Cobwebs in every corner
Shaking in the wind.
Faces in the windows
Piercing eyes stare you down.
The windows crash open and closed.
The curtains desolate and suffering.
The garden overgrown,
Tangled with ivy.
Rot is slowly becoming part of the house,
Sinking its way into the wood.
Gates stand tall as if to protect the house
Yet they are rusted and old.
My thirst for knowledge
Brought me one step too far.
I wonder will I ever get out?

Lily Rooney (13)
St Paul's RC College, Burgess Hill

ALONE

Alone, I sit on my chair
Seeing kids run here and there
Wish I could be one of them
I used to be, way back then.
The fun we had, laughing all day
Then I was the one who had to pay.
It's not my fault I have a big mouth,
But she had to do it, she kicked me out.
But I guess that was my choice, to be alone,
There never was a grand throne.
I want to come back and laugh like we did,
But how can I, I'm just a kid.
I could never tell someone, pick up the phone
Because I really am just
Alone.

Joseph Carter (12)
St Paul's RC College, Burgess Hill

HEROES

Heroes live to die, never understanding why there can't just be peace,
Never our choice, never our decision, even if they are to be deceased,
For any soldier or private, their lives are lived to save the lives of others
And us, we don't acknowledge the heroism of these people
Or the pain of the families and mothers,
Heroes are the unknown souls that rest in the deserted, barren land,
Who fought for their country, now may never stand,
Why war?
What do we have to be fighting for?
All these soldiers fighting for their lives,
Only to leave their loved ones and wives,
Heroes need recognition,
But that is just my opinion.

Caitlin Roberts (16)
The Angmering School, Littlehampton

DEAR OLD FRIEND

Dear old friend
The memories we shared
Through times of hardship,
We grinned and bared

Through bombs and pain
Keep our heads high did we
Your war is over
You're finally free

From the age of but ten
In old London town
We ran wild and loose
No one dared hold us down

Arrived home late every night
After supper, we played
It was all we knew,
We did it our way

Through German blitz
And panic for years
We held strong for each other
And we held back the tears

For now, my old pal
It's time for farewell
No more struggles or anguish
No more bullets shall you shell

Goodbye and good luck
Every journey must end
I'll remember ours always
Dear old friend.

Marcus Nicholas Bird (16)
The Angmering School, Littlehampton

EDUCATION

You're studying. Writing equations, persuasions, learning about the Afghan invasion,
You look across to your best friend, Nathan, and whisper, 'I'm so bored.'
Looking for a quick escape from reality, but he tells you, 'You need to change your mentality.'
You turn around and continue turning to insanity,
As you think and wonder, 'What's my brain capacity?'
Wondering how much you can really learn,
How many facts, figures, dates and digits can you really remember before you go over your limit?

But then your mind fidgets, craving knowledge,
'Why do I accept and acknowledge, that my grade defines me at college?'
You return to the last question, what do I have to do this session?
Looking at your to-do list, your worn, dog-eared list,
But around your brain is a thick layer of mist.
You crumple your paper into your fist, you insist you'll work.
If you kept it up, you'd someday be a clerk or a teacher or designer or something with good money, because to put it bluntly, that's all that matters.
Your mind chatters, asking questions, finding your place, but that's not how you should be using this space.

You're always asking the point, but never speaking it.
You get a bit angry. As you question the point of revising,
But you change. You're rising, you're not here to be defined by a letter.
You're better than a score, better than a grade. The doubts in your mind are beginning to fade as A, B, C and D simply become history, you stand up for something more.
You're going to stop treating this like a chore. If one door closes, another one opens,
You're going to smash down that door and speak the words unspoken,
Because you shouldn't believe, in something so broken.

For the wannabe bankers, and the 'BTEC *******',
the nerds, the drop-outs, the ones with set futures and the ones with

the doubts,
When something is wrong we stand up for it, so put down your script
and use your true wit.

It's time you stood up, alongside your peers, your nation,
To change the way, we think of education.

Liam Gilbey (17)
The Angmering School, Littlehampton

SUN RAYS

The sunlight shone down into my eyes,
It took me to another world,
Fireflies danced around the sun like it was its king,
The lord's servants flew me up to the highest point,
His sunrays glowed through the evil monster's minions,

I finally caught him in my jar,
I gently opened the lid and *fizz, pop,*
It smelt of Tango orange with a hint of sweetness,
Suddenly, it disappeared and ran through my body.
I felt the rush of joy in my soul.

The darkness had come upon us,
Engulfing all happiness and fun,
Until I come along making people feel warm inside,
I attack the joy sucker and it was gone.

It was a rainy and horrible day,
I had no joy left in me,
The beast inside me roared,
I was outside.
The friend inside me disappeared,
The sun had burnt my heart,
It was dripping down my eyes,
And it was gone . . .

Jack Chapman (12)
The Angmering School, Littlehampton

SAD

What fascinates me most,
Is how the face changes when the heart knows sorrow.
When the mirror tells more stories
Than the brain can admit to.
Others notice it before you do
But it hits with force.
It's all consuming.
Enveloping heart,
Conquering mind.
Undermining every decision.
Destabilising ordinary function.
Vivacity decays,
And despondency flourishes.

Their enquiries can never be satisfied,
For your own desire to know is so strong,
So fundamental to the issue,
That it becomes the problem itself.
Clouding the mind,
Inhibiting progress,
Catalysing the descent into darkness.
Obstructing the way out.
Burning the ladder,
Rung by rung,
Tear by tear.

Nobody helps or comforts,
All of them masters in sophisticated ignorance.
Soon what was once relevant
Transforms into dismal irrelevancy.
The difference between joy and dejection,
Is greater than it's ever been before.
It doesn't make sense.
The answer cannot be ascertained.
It can't be bought in a pharmacy.

It can't be found at the bottom of a bottle.
It can't be snorted or smoked.
No, it's transcendent.

Charlie James Douglas Batchelor (18)
The Angmering School, Littlehampton

WILL DODGE

A man called Will Dodge,
lived in a ski lodge.
Life in the mountains was lonely,
he found that he had only
his Batman movie box set for company.

After watching for an hour or so,
he came to discover that he wasn't alone.
The characters came to life on the screen
and started shouting things that he thought were mean.

His past had come back to haunt him,
memories of which were rather grim.
He didn't want to believe it,
the murders couldn't have been him.

But they were.
He slew all those who looked down on him
and his way of life.
The bullies caused him so much pain and strife
so he slashed them all with a Swiss army knife,
only to be sent away for eternity.

This place was no sky lodge.
But to poor old Will Dodge,
his mental state had gone away.
In a straight jacket he would stay.
A life sentence he is to serve
for a crime, some would say,
the bullies deserved.

Louis Haste (16)
The Angmering School, Littlehampton

ON A SUMMER'S EVENING, LATE

On a summer's evening, late,
Where the whispers first appear,
Where the woodlands come to life,
Humanity disappears.

Only one human knows,
Understands as she grows,
First when the wind bellowed,
She was called Willow.

On a summer's evening, late,
The whispers first appeared,
Willow stood near,
Whistling voices,
And ferocious roars,
The woods came alive,
To talk and thrive.

They became her friends,
They laughed and joked around,
The more she came,
The more friends she found.

All this time she spent,
On this summer's evening late.

These late summer nights,
Went flashing by,
Those horrid woodmen were bad men.

Those summer evening lates,
Where the whispers appeared,
Now disappeared,
Left Willow,
In sorrow
And solitude.

Jasmine Payne (12)
The Angmering School, Littlehampton

THE POETRY TRIALS - HAMPSHIRE & SUSSEX

JUDGING BY APPEARANCES

A smattering of make-up parades across her face,
Lurid colours, natural yet fake, designed to make
All the boys turn their heads. But she talks, flirts
With them all, in different manners for each.
They think they're the only one but her mask
Deceives them well. Her powdered mask.

The aged man, held in awe as he tells
Stories of supreme valour, heroics and might.
Pride in his years, gun held in hand. Ordering
His subordinates to great victory. Cleansed medals
Glinting on his chest like steel blades in harsh sun.
How many mothers' children did he sacrifice?

Respected banker. Her neat hair tied, nails manicured.
Audits, statements pass before the icy fire
Residing in her eyes, like subjects before a monarch.
Her decisions are emotionless, her word
A decree, set in stone. All are at her mercy.
Balancing the books, never making a loss.

Standing in the pub, beer mug in hand.
His loud, booming voice, of cheer and authority,
Reaching his friends. Confidence radiates,
Hence the admiration from them. As he stands
Firmly, asserting. An incredible man. But his wife
Does not think so. Not with her bruises.

Quiet and reserved in her four-walled home.
Her life gradually slips, from beneath two
Layers of home-knitted cardigans. Long forgotten.
But in her prime a majestic figure as she
Negotiated the aircraft to landing while
Being bombarded. Never faltering. Saving lives.

Ben Simpson (17)
The Angmering School, Littlehampton

DROWNING

I'm drowning,
drowning in the crowds of people that surround me as I struggle for breath, drowning.
Trapped in a state of fear as their eyes pierce my skin.
I'm drowning,
I won't survive,
I'm going to drown
I can't do this.
Thoughts rush through my mind,
as if they were racehorses galloping around a track.
I can't turn away.
I can't turn back.
I can't do this.
My emotions run wild as waves envelop my mind,
dragging my soul down
towards a desolate ocean bed.
I want to be like they are,
joyful, confident.
I want to feel like they do,
hopeful, brave.
Attacks like these only last a moment,
yet they feel like an eternity.
Over as soon as they begin,
all I want is to fit in.
I'm drowning.
No one hears my cries for help as I fall,
deeper and deeper.
Soon I'll rise again
And I'll be stronger than before.
These panics can't control me.
I'm drowning.

Chloe Paisley (14)
The Angmering School, Littlehampton

THE WATER SUCCESSION

My cycle began in the bath,
When I came out of a tap.
It was such a good laugh,
And now I need a nap.

And then I was evaporating,
My particles were set free.
I was recuperating,
Oh yes! I need a cup of tea.

And then I was condensed,
My freedom was lost.
So I returned my common sense,
It all came at a cost.

And then I got back in the bath,
I flowed down the plughole.
Nothing could get in my path,
This was my final goal.

And then I was in the ocean,
I found within myself an emo.
I downed the deep, blue potion,
So I found little Nemo.

Sophie Baker (14)
The Angmering School, Littlehampton

THE ELECTRIC LIGHT

Hanging there from the ceiling, the electric light,
Shimmering with beauty, the electric light,
Too cool for school, the electric light,
The ceiling departs revealing, the electric light,
It reveals the objects under the darkness, the electric light,
It's in my heart, the electric light,
It's like the sun, the electric light,
The switch is majestic of . . . the electric light!

Toby Hother (14)
The Angmering School, Littlehampton

THE WOLF AND THE OWL

Marshmallow soft
It sticks under his feet
As he pads along to where the trees and snow meet
At the pearl glow of the moon he lets out a howl
At the corner of his eye
White feathers fly
When he sees yellow eyes he knows it's an owl

It hoots and tweets
It repeats and repeats
It waits for his prey
The same way every day
The sky is grey until the crescent moon comes out
When it does he tweets and pouts
When the wolf howls again it's time to go
Then they swoop and run together in the snow.

Amy Wilson (11)
The Angmering School, Littlehampton

SHADOWS

They seep elegantly across the ground,
The spectacular sun melting over the awakening village.
Shadows begin to gradually shrink away
As the sun gets swallowed by a blanket of cloud,
Like they are lethargic animals drifting off to sleep.

Rip. It tears.
The golden dragon bursts through the clouds,
Heaving a breath of light.
Restlessly, all of the shadows awaken
And a cup of them spills all around me.
I see them galloping contentedly,
Grasping onto the ankles of the smiling children in front.
It is glorious.

Sophie Wayman (11)
The Angmering School, Littlehampton

SUNLIGHT

A silent ray of sunlight tans my pale skin
I reach out and catch the piece of happiness
My heart flips with joy and warmth
And brings butterflies into my stomach

It feels like honey, warm and sticky
Some manages to escape and flies into my mouth
The delightful taste of summer hangs onto my tongue
And my body goes numb

The diamonds glisten on the river surface
They're tempting me to go in the water
Without letting go of the beauty, I dive in
I open my hands . . . and sorrow flips my stomach.

Emma Needle (11)
The Angmering School, Littlehampton

THE FOREST OF FIRE

In the screamingly dark forest with no one in sight,
A trail of fire crawls up my body,
Empowering inside my soul.

A spark of anger triggers
The fire-breathing dragon inside me.

In the pitch-black night,
My body glows into an eye-catching fireball,
Stunning anyone or anything into a deep, fiery sleep.

Crawling to the depths of the stream,
I try to rub out every speck of sunlight but instead,
I never return . . .

Lily Tamara Wells (12)
The Angmering School, Littlehampton

MY GLOWING SUN

I will climb the frozen mountain
To get the glowing sun
Into my glass jar.
When I pour the sunlight
Onto my hands
It feels elastic, sticky and hot.
The sun smells like lemon and honeycomb.
If I wash my sunlight
In the silver sink
It will sparkle
Look like golden brown caramel.

Jagoda Iwanska (11)
The Angmering School, Littlehampton

THE FIREBALL IN SPACE

Moonlight filled the jar
But it needs sunlight,
fire burst out the rocket
As it lifted off into space.
Darkness filled space
But there was a massive fireball
The only light source.
The jar was full
Of magnificent light.
Thank you, sun,
Thank you.

Alex Furniss (11)
The Angmering School, Littlehampton

SUNLIGHT

The light wears anything
Like a jacket on its back
It can wear moss that's green
Or a rock with a crack
The light wears you like
A suit
But the light can die
And it starts to go dark
But never worry
It's never far.

Thomas Hartigan (11)
The Angmering School, Littlehampton

THE MOON

The moon is a pearl
that glistens white
high up in the sky.

Its luminous glow
streaks down upon the Earth
and fills the night sky with light.

Waxing and waning,
but always silent.
Ever present, every night.

Oliver Fullbrook (11)
The Angmering School, Littlehampton

WINTER WONDERLAND

A city of sirens left with no sound
So rural less urban
The snowflakes brush the ground,

Street lights like soldiers
Defeated by a blanket of snow
The white is bright amongst the dim glow,

Children slide across the frosted mirror
The works of a winter night
They sway and play and disappear out of sight.

Holly Parisi (16)
The Angmering School, Littlehampton

THE WITCH'S CACKLE

Long ago on a Halloween night
A witch's cackle made a fright.
From north to south surrounded the noise,
As tick by tock, the beat of a clock.
Screeching sounds came closer to my ear
As ... *crash, bang, wallop!*
The witch appeared!

A puff of smoke, a trickle of blood
1,000 warts and a broomstick.
There she was.
'Mwhahahahah!'
With the witch's long, gritty nails,
She grabbed the sweets from the dear children.
Tears and trickles ran down their faces
As the witch vanished away.

On the 31st October, every Halloween night,
If you listen carefully
You can still hear the haunting sounds of the witch's cackle,
'Mwhahahah!'

Isabel Cosgrove (12)
The Costello School, Basingstoke

BUDDY

Winter mornings with steam escaping
From my nose and mouth.
Putting on boots and gloves
To keep me warm.
Hugging my arms to my chest
To keep in the heat
As I walk down the frozen track
To his stable.
Nearing the stables I hear
Impatient hooves telling me to hurry.
Buddy jerks his head
Neighing a greeting
Nuzzling my hands for a hidden treat.
Breakfast over, tackle on
We head to the countryside.
Trotting out across the frosty track
Buddy and I alone
With only the occasional falling leaf
For company.
Trotting, cantering, then galloping fast
Tendrils of steam escaping
From Buddy's flared nostrils.
Galloping, feeling free.
With the cold wind in my face
Taking my breath
And making my eyes water.
Back at the stables
Feeling exhilarated from the ride
And cold.
I sponge off the sweat
And groom out mud
And loose hair from his coat.
Buddy nuzzles my pockets
Checking for forgotten treats,
Before I turn him out
Into the field for a well earned rest.

Charlotte Rebecca Hill (15)
The Costello School, Basingstoke

IF I KNEW

If only I knew how it's going to be
If only when I try to fix things,
They became better
If only I was certain of how others feel
And if only people believed what I say . . .

If I knew how to show what I really feel
If I knew how to make people understand
If I knew how to make them believe
If I knew how to make them happy

If making people happy doesn't leave
Me sad
If making them understand doesn't make
Me an ignorant
If making them believe doesn't make me
A liar
And if letting them know how I feel doesn't
Leave me numb

Things would've never reached that point
I know I would be in a much happier place
No one would be in a much happier place
No one would ever blame me for not
Thinking

That's life . . . you're never certain
You never know, you're never sure
You're not going to live that dream of yours
And life would never be 'trouble free'
You have to live with what you have
You try to fix the broken glass
You try to collect the shattered
Pieces
You make the best of every day

It's like a train that never stops
Keep going through life without
Pausing
Just live each day and throw
It behind you
Don't look back or you'll break
Your neck!

Taine Macleod Peacock (14)
The Costello School, Basingstoke

ONLY DANCERS WILL UNDERSTAND

Only dancers will understand,
The need to dance at every location,
The feelings you get when any song plays,
It's an unstoppable drive,
An indescribable sensation.

Only dancers will get
That feeling of pride when you move up a grade,
Or getting that distinction you've always wanted,
The emotional day of getting your first medal,
Oh, dreams have been made.

Only dancers will remember,
Their beginning knock or tumble,
That crushing fact of defeat and failure,
It's basically the end of the world,
And you'll never erase that stumble.

Only dancers will understand,
Those overwhelming moments as you wait backstage,
Heart racing, hands shaking,
But as you stand there, adrenaline filling the air,
The thought hits you,

You will always treasure this passion
And carry it everywhere,
No matter your age.

Charlotte Harfield
The Costello School, Basingstoke

THERE'S NO SMOKE WITHOUT FIRE

Rushing through the hallways,
Leaping in the air,
Bony fingers longing,
Screams and squeals are rare.

Spreading like a virus,
Crawling under doors,
Grabbing for its victims,
Seeping through the floors.

The burning scent arises,
The woman starts to stir,
'Wake up now.
It's not too late.
You could escape unhurt.'

Flames - they flicker,
Listen - they hiss - *sssss* . . .
These weeps of those who didn't survive
A sound of guilt you'll never miss.

Well, she did.

Soon she'll join those dreadful weeps,
Her voice distinct and clear,
Mute those screams but then
There still remains the fear.

Watch her now as she sleeps so sweetly,
Unaware as the blaze stumbles closer,
Lighting up the dismal room,
Igniting it with amber and fuschia.

Her slumber stops and she awakes,
Only to realise it's too late and,
As the smoke envelopes her eyelids,
She sleeps again.

Screams and squeals are rare,
Yet by day grow in volume.

Millicent Crass (14)
The Costello School, Basingstoke

THE BEACH

I relaxed my tensed body and breathed in the salty air around me.
The gentle sea breeze blew against my face peacefully.
The happiness inside me gleamed and I was urged to smile.
My anxious spirits are set free,
When I am alone.

The golden, soft sand massaged my pink toes.
A tingle of joy crept up my spine.
I forgot about my past and just imagined what was going to happen in my future.
I suddenly feel like nothing matters,
When I am alone.

The white, oblivious seagulls soared around and above my head
Like red, cunning kites, about to dive for their prey.
For the first time ever, little gormless kids screeching in the sea
Did not bother me.
Nothing can destroy my happiness,
When I am alone.

I closed my eyes but I could still smell the salty sea air tingling my nostrils.
My mind had drifted off to another magical dimension,
Despite alarming noises going off around me.
The bright sunlight beamed on my trembling skin
Like a white angel looking down at me from the wonderful heavens.
I can imagine whatever I like,
When I am alone.

I never want to forget that feeling.
It will be treasured in my mind forever!
I waited, I watched, I wondered;
Something dark and shadowy was coming slowly towards me.
Suddenly,
I was not alone . . .

Freya Barter (12)
The Costello School, Basingstoke

NOTHING

The empty space
Just there
It has no use
But to sit there
Wondering, waiting, watching
Until it is something

It watches us
Like a hawk
To steal our thoughts
Hopeless while it is
Wondering, waiting, watching
Until it is something

A lonely figure
Just lying there
Not moving, nor motionless
It is sad and craves us, while it is
Wondering, waiting, watching
Until it is something

It feels our happiness
Sitting in the blank space
Crying without tears
It feels hatred, envy and carries on
Wondering, waiting, watching
Until it is something

It rises
To life
It is happy
Now the time has come
It doesn't need to wonder, wait or watch
Because it is something.

Ryan Baker (11)
The Costello School, Basingstoke

THE POETRY TRIALS - HAMPSHIRE & SUSSEX

... 5, 6, 7, 8

Some sit inside and watch TV
While others use the music
To help them set free
They turn, leap and glide through the air
She's so beautiful
You can't help but stare
As you walk in the room
You can already sense it
The power all comes
From where the pen sits
You take a breath
And think back to the times
That you stand on stage
Not needing a light to shine
Memories flash back
From your first lesson
Crying in the corner
As others take an impression
Now the little ones
Look up to you all
As you move so quickly
But still fail to fall
Ten long years
You've been playing this game
After this exam
It will never be the same
You take your place centre stage
As the music starts
Your life writes another page
... 5, 6, 7, 8.

Amy Regan
The Costello School, Basingstoke

SHOULD I BE THERE?

Am I here?
Do you see me?
Or am I just a shadow,
Always steps behind you
In this life I follow?

But can you call it a life?
A life with no living
Is a life with no living, a life at all?
My heart beats,
But it's ice cold.

Some think I'm moody,
Some think I'm sad.
They blame it on hormones,
That I'd be glad.
But no meds or potions can fix this pain,
The pain I feel with nothing to blame.

Trapped in my own life.
6 o'clock
7 o'clock
10 o'clock
Bed!
I'm a zombie walking,
May as well be dead.

Time!
It's against me.
It seems to last forever.
How about I end it in the next half hour?

Katie Jeffery
The Costello School, Basingstoke

THE POETRY TRIALS - HAMPSHIRE & SUSSEX

TIME TICKING

Time ticking, and ticking
I sit here
Time ticking, and ticking
I sit here, wondering
Time ticking, and ticking
I sit here
Wondering
Thinking about if I was there
I sit here
Time ticking, still ticking
Thinking about if I was with her
Time ticking, still ticking
My thoughts engulf me
I can't shake the fact that
Time's still ticking
Faster
I look for aid
Even faster
Wondering again
Even faster
What if I was there?
I rise up
Begin to walk
My thoughts - interrupted
A gold flick of hair
Time stopped just ticking
It was Her.

Alex Danylyuk (14)
The Costello School, Basingstoke

THE POET FROM HONG KONG

There once was a man from Hong Kong,
Whose poems were always too long.
When I asked why this was,
He said, 'It's because
The last line keeps going on and on and on and on...'

His poems spread wide and far,
They even went into a bar.
The first person who heard it
Shouted the verdict,
Then he was aggressively debarred.

When the sad-man walked home,
(Which was shaped like a dome),
He walked through the door;
Could take it no more,
But was relieved he was all on his own.

Alone in his bed,
There were thoughts in his head,
He wrote down a verse,
Then began to rehearse,
Excited about his job he began to race ahead.

There once was a man from Hong Kong,
Whose poems were always too long,
When I asked why this was,
He said, 'It's because
The last line kept going on and on and on and on.'

Hugh Sergeant
The Costello School, Basingstoke

HARRY KANE, HE'S ONE OF OUR OWN

Harry Kane, he's one of our own,
Harry Kane, he's one of our own,
He shoots, he scores,
He's one of our own.

Harry Kane, he's one of our own,
Harry Kane, he's one of our own,
He scores a hat trick,
He's one of our own.

Harry Kane, he's one of our own,
Harry Kane, he's one of our own,
And he plays for Tottenham,
He's one of our own.

Harry Kane, he's one of our own,
Harry Kane, he's one of our own,
He's number 10,
He's one of our own.

Harry Kane, he's one of our own,
Harry Kane, he's one of our own,
Now everyone wants him,
He's one of our own.

Harrison Keast (11)
The Costello School, Basingstoke

HALLOWEEN TERROR

On a Halloween night,
The stars shone bright,
As they went from door to door,
Getting lots of candy to stuff themselves galore,
However, there is one problem,
Which they have totally ignored,
Don't get me wrong, they knew not,
The mistake they have just made,
But a mistake like this, oh dear, oh dear,
Could take them to the grave.

As they walked down the alley,
They suddenly jumped with fright,
When they saw a woman,
Shrieking with all her might.
Her hand grabbed them, other fist clenched,
And the girls realised what they had done,
Gone to the alley of death.

They screamed and screamed,
And screeched and screeched,
Until they escaped her grasp.
They ran until their legs couldn't take it,
They fell into their front door, at last.

Phoebe Mahoney (11)
The Costello School, Basingstoke

THE HORROR OF WAR

A hiss of gas, the soldiers choke,
They cannot see through all the smoke,
Blood and guts spray the ground,
Rotting corpses lie around.
A beating heart,
A severed head,
Haunting symbols of the dead.
Bodies pile on No-Man's-Land,
Blood on every trooper's hands.
Bones are broken,
Blood is spilled,
Everybody's getting killed.
Vital organs line the floor,
Remember, remember,
All the gore.

'War, pain and suffering,
Much worse than a video
Buffering.'

Joe Duerden (14)
The Costello School, Basingstoke

A PERFECT TEN

Pulling back, I feel the tension on the string,
The bending of the wood,
I aim for my target,
Straight for the gold.
My mind begins to wander to memories long forgotten,
To times of things that should never have happened.
The phantom echo of pain rings through my mind.
I try to remember a happy time,
But there are none to find.
I breathe,
First in, then out.
Reminding that those times are done.
Remembering where I am.
I redraw,
Close my eyes and release.
Opening my eyes, I approach the arrow,
A perfect 10.
Ripping out the arrow,
Roughly wiping tears that were not there before.
Walking away,
I wait for the end.

Natalie Gay
The Costello School, Basingstoke

HALLOWEEN

H aunted house
A pple bobbing
L aughing, screaming, having fun
L ightning, thunder, there could be some
O wls hooting in the dark
W olves howling in the park
E ngraved pumpkins big and small
E agle eyes are watching all
N ight-night, sweet dreams.

Thomas Barton (11)
The Costello School, Basingstoke

THE POETRY TRIALS - HAMPSHIRE & SUSSEX

POETRY?

Once there was a paper clip
Wait . . . that's not it.
Once there was - wait - oh, never mind.
Poems are tricky,
That's all I have to say.
And now there's nothing that rhymes with tricky . . .
Great!
What rhymes with 'say'?
And now 'great'.
Wait . . . 'great' rhymes with 'great'
And 'say' rhymes with 'say'.
Does that make me a poet?

So, since I'm now a poet, I'll give you a tester,
Though I think I'm a jester
In the poem world.

I can drive people round the bend,
And send them on their way to their wits' end.
But poetry?
Naah . . .
I think I'll leave it to the experts.

Isobel Reid (11)
The Costello School, Basingstoke

MIDNIGHT

I wake
I listen
I hear
I feel a shiver down my spine
I turn
I see
I stop
I scream!

Elliot Turner (12)
The Costello School, Basingstoke

THE CLIMB UP THE MOUNTAIN

As I climb further up the mountain
I start to lose my breath and stop for a minute
I look at my surroundings
I see a land of beautiful creatures and magical colours
Around me are birds of all shades of blue and green
These are the moments that stay with you for a lifetime.

As I climb further up the mountain
The strain on my body is getting more intense
But I have to carry on to achieve my goal
I've gone so far now, I can't quit
The other climbers are making it look easy
But for me it's not!

As I climb further up the mountain
I'm joined by other climbers
They're giving me weird looks
How did they get up here so fast?
And why aren't they using equipment?
After all, this is Mount Crabtree!

Callum McKeaveney
The Costello School, Basingstoke

SLEEP

Morning light shines through the gaps in my curtains,
It's early for certain,
I am really tired,
More sleep required.
I drag myself out of bed,
Walking into the kitchen to be fed.
I finish my breakfast at last,
My mum shouts, 'Why aren't you in bed?'
'You're up too early,' she said.
So I didn't have to get out of bed,
'Oh well,' that's what I said.

Ben Matthews (14)
The Costello School, Basingstoke

FRIENDSHIP

Friendship is like a magical bond,
Talking and chatting like a fish bubbling away in a pond.
Being crazy and funny with my friends just makes me free,
All of our memories will be carried along with me.

Whenever I'm feeling sad or down,
I know my friends can cheer me up by acting like clowns.
We may fight,
But our friendship will still shine like a light.

Going in different directions,
Please, may our friendship not experience any reactions,
Making friends along the way,
I hope our friendship will still stay.

Endless laughter, I hope it never ends,
That's just why I love being your friend.

Warm-hearted friendships,
Will come your way and share good times,
Such a lovely day!

Kaviya Balasritharan
The Costello School, Basingstoke

JUST A WINDOW

I was just a window;
I was translucent to all,
But I had emotions until then.

I remember being locked up,
Having to stand in one single place,
Not able to move.

I remember seeing you tucked up in bed,
While my job was to battle with Mother Nature,
My only goal was to keep you safe.

I remember seeing you clambering up the old oak,
Branch by branch,
He was my only friend.
While I was worrying for you
As I had no arms to catch with.

I remember the last time I saw you,
Happily skipping into the school bus,
No one knew what was to come . . .

Erin Onel Edgar (12)
The Costello School, Basingstoke

THE POETRY TRIALS - HAMPSHIRE & SUSSEX

BACKSTAGE BUTTERFLIES

Backstage,
Hands are shaking,
Been waiting for an age.
Butterflies awakening,
Flying on my inside.

Flying, swirling,
Making me feel ill.
My teacher saying,
'The audience's seats have been filled.'
This comment wasn't helping.
I felt the butterflies rising
To the back of my throat, they're coming.

But now the curtain is rising,
The lights are blinding,
My face is smiling.
The music is starting
And my butterflies are gone!

Amy Kent (11)
The Costello School, Basingstoke

WHAT IF I TOLD YOU IT WAS HEAVEN AND HELL

Some smile, others cry
Some are just in denial
If you smiled at me one more time
Would it make me feel like my once upon a time
Or was it just a lie?
Media portrays love as endless happiness
Something that everyone is destined to have
Maybe you were scared to live life alone
And didn't want to be home alone
What if you were just insecure
And didn't want to do this anymore?
It kills when I look into your eyes
And know you've been telling me endless lies.

I'm fed up of trying to make you understand
Maybe you were not in my life plan . . .

Chelsea-Marie Cochrane
The Costello School, Basingstoke

I'M NOT THE GIRL WHO . . .

I'm not the girl who is patient.
I'm not the girl who holds back.
But I'm not the girl who deceives you
And I'm not the girl who will smack.

I'm not the girl who is dainty,
I'm not the girl who will cry.
But I'm not the girl who will hate you,
And I'm not the girl who walks by.

I'm not the girl who is pretty,
I'm not the girl who is slim.
But I'm not the girl who is unworthy
And I never mean to sin.

Erica Van Den Ordel (15)
The Costello School, Basingstoke

AUTUMN POEM

Walking through the depressed rain,
Empty streets, no sign of kids on my way,
I get stopped by the beautiful nature.
Red, orange, brown and grey,
Oh, it is a miserable day.

Foggy mornings, damp, cold and grey,
Nature's blanket covering the day.
Shorter days, frosty and wet,
Winter's round the corner but not quite yet.

And just a quick thing before you go,
I'll be collecting what you have left.

Winter is round the corner
And it's already getting colder.
One last thing before you go,
I'll be right here till the next fall will come.

Delia Gheorghe
The Costello School, Basingstoke

HALLOWEEN

On the most spooky night of your life,
Was the howl of the night,
Skeletons come alive for the night,
And give everyone a jolly big fright.

Spooky, scary skeletons,
Come from the graveyard,
Come out on the streets,
Waiting for defeat,
The humans wait.

The purge comes alive,
The people try to survive,
Lock the doors,
Stay inside.

Keira Purver (11)
The Costello School, Basingstoke

WHAT MATTERS TO ME

I do a bend,
I do a twirl,
I do a routine that makes people hurl.
Handstands are straight,
Cartwheels are great,
People may hate but haters will hate.
When I do my routine,
People may stare,
They may wonder,
'Why does she care?'
But overall,
Deep inside,
I care because I care,
No matter where.
So here's a poem about gymnastics,
But overall it's about what matters.

Megan Temple-Nidd (12)
The Costello School, Basingstoke

BULLY POEM

Just because you have more friends,
You make me cry, my happiness ends.
Be yourself, don't let anyone change you,
You're perfect and beautiful, love yourself like I do.
Don't let bullies get you down,
Turn your unhappy life around.
You should be smiling, being happy,
But you're sat alone, with bullies being snappy.
Just keep your head held up high
And wave to those bullies, goodbye!
So keep a big smile on your face,
Do you see now?
You're perfect, don't listen to those bullies!
What do they know?

Brioni Fayter
The Costello School, Basingstoke

I'M LOVIN' IT

McDonald's, take a look, feast your eyes,
Only one thirty-nine for large fries,
Not going there only results in cries,
Food so good, no need for lies.
Cheeseburger, mayo chicken, crunchie McFlurry,
Grab a couple of quid, you'll need to hurry.
Never a rip-off, no need to worry,
Food so good, brings a smile to Andy Murray.
Big Mac, chicken nuggets, Happy Meals,
Go there if you're looking for good deals.
When you leave it brings out the feels.
Food so good, they never serve eels,
McDonald's, take a look feast your eyes . . .
I'm lovin' it.

Ollie Pegg
The Costello School, Basingstoke

ANIMAL CRUELTY

A nimals having to face fear, being
N eglected
I felt so alone
M iserable
A nd
L ooking after itself or nothing

C an't last on nothing for long
R eally nothing to rely on
U nloved and dying
E quality
L ife being wasted away
T he blood surrounding
Y es, can we stop this now.

Becki Giggs
The Costello School, Basingstoke

GUNSHOTS - A WW2 POEM

Gunshots
The soldiers charged
Through the splattering of lead.
Sorrow all around
One by one they fell
But their spirit never died.

Into the jaws of death
They charge, gunshots
Were against them but
Never did they look back.
One by one they fell
But never did their spirit fade
Not even today.

William Colegate
The Costello School, Basingstoke

CRICKET TIME

The bowler throws the ball.
The batter hits the ball.
Ball charges like a bull.
A fielder caught the ball.

Fielder throws the ball, then *bang!*
Ball hits stumps, batter out.
New batter.
Bowler's ready to throw.

Bowler throws, batter swings.
The ball shoots round the pitch.
Run batter, go fielders.
Can he win? Yes, he has.

Alexander De Silva (11)
The Costello School, Basingstoke

BOXING POEM - UNTIL THE END

Boxing is strength
Boxing is power

Great sport with lots of good people
Non-stop fighting
Every night

Very tired
It's never getting old!

Never give up
Keep fighting until the end

My wraps go on
Never coming off

Ding, ding, echoes fill 'my' ring
Crowd goes crazy cheering and clapping!

Liquid pours from his eyes
Swollen and in pain

He's never leaving.

Harrison Konieczny (12)
The Forest School, Horsham

A SEASONAL LIPOGRAM

When the trees rose, when the rivers flowed; I did not stop still
When the green fields grew, when the sheep flocked; I did not stop still
Whilst the sun peered down on me, like weights on my spine; I could not rest;
I could not be finished
Whilst the few clouds in the sky idle by, in their positions;
I could not rest; I could not be finished
Despite the cool breeze blowing; I did not feel the cold,
Despite the tumble greenery, dropping from the trees; I did not feel the cold,
When the winter months brought closure to the troublesome twelve-month cycle,
I feel the time to rest, to stop, to look, to rest,
To feel the breeze on my shoulders.
Now I feel the minutes left to enjoy it.

Nathan Kettle
The Forest School, Horsham

SNOWFALL

(A Lipogram - T)

Gracefully falling down
Preparing for a new home
Dazzling colours sparkling and shining
Middle of fun and games
Children screaming and laughing as I soar in the face of a surprised child
Life is nearly ending
Sparkling sun absorbs all life
Rising up in a barren place
Warming up, joining my family
We fall as liquid once again
Beginning a new escapade...

David Ironmonger
The Forest School, Horsham

COLOURS

(A Lipogram - A)

Red is fiery.
Fierce bolts of thunder plunging into your body.
See how it rises from the fire,
jumping and bounding.

Vermillion is glowing.
Its touch fills you with bliss.
It kisses you fervently,
its cheeks truly snuggly.

Yellow is joyous.
Visions of contentment.
The world where depression,
possesses no concern.

Green is new.
Sprouting from the undergrowth.
Developing unique lives for everyone to cherish,
extensive plus diminutive.

Blue is sorrowful.
Immersing people in pitiful grief.
Distress besides woe,
is everything they know.

White is free.
Letting your mind flourish.
Untold mysteries to be uncovered,
throughout words and expressions.

Ebony is unnerving.
One murky, gloomy mess.
Towering over you like fingers edging,
closer, closer ...

Rachael Locke (12)
The Gregg School, Southampton

LOOKING UP

(A Lipogram - A)

Looking up into the inky sky
glittering, glistening, tiny dots.
Remote.
Hope with wonder, joy with sorrow,
ivory with ebony, good with evil.
Looking up.

Looking up to the brighter side,
inspire merriment not grief.
The brighter side is the best side,
don't let yourself be pulled down.
Keep positive.
Looking up.

Looking for support,
nurture beside love.
Held in such high esteem,
their words become soft whispers.
Invisible.
Looking up.

Glowing embers dimming,
shrinking down to nothing.
Soon they will be lit once more,
filled with new fuel, new hope.
Looking up.

Holly Beadsworth (12)
The Gregg School, Southampton

FUDGE

(A Lipogram - A)

I looked for the luxurious sweet, I found it!
Hidden in mounds of other glorious sweets.
My mouth trembled with excitement.
The glistening, golden bundle held my fudge.
The bundle, shiny plus glossy,
Rustled gently when I touched it,
I could not control my hunger.
I opened the glimmering bundle,
My mouth couldn't survive without the rich, soothing delight.
It seemed endless.
I closed my eyes,
Popped the sweet into my mouth.
My teeth delved into the velvety goodness.
My mouth burst with zingy deliciousness!
The delight, chewy, gooey, sticky,
Everything luscious confectionery should be.
I devoured the sweet,
I felt the soothing texture running down inside me.
It reminded me of pure bliss.
How could you dislike something so divine?
Succeeding my blissful consumption I devoured numerous more,
However the more I demolished,
The more sickly they grew.
Until in the end I needed to stop.

Emily Kerry (13)
The Gregg School, Southampton

SEASIDE

(A Lipogram - T)

Waves crashing forcefully on rocks,
Children swimming around,
Seagulls swooping up above,
Screeching loud cries for food,
Golden warm sand,
Skimming rocks,
Chips being munched on,
Ice cream as well,
Children climbing over rocks,
Crabs clicking claws,
Blown-up beach balls,
Rugby
And volleyballs,
Shells clinging on rocks,
Kids rock pooling, observing fish,
Ships sailing far away,
Surfers riding waves all day,
And endless valley of golden sand,
Children playing hand-in-hand,
Holiday homes close for few,
Holiday homes have lovely views,
Beach shops selling goods,
Fishermen hoping for big fish.

Henry Gates (11)
The Gregg School, Southampton

BUTTERFLIES

(A Lipogram - A)

Their soft, flowing wings never touch the ground,
Their wings glitter like jewels in the summer sun,
Twirling, whirling, looking for fun.
Once one went down onto my fingertip,
It surprised me extremely with its trembling cry,
It trembled, I stroked, I giggled with glee,
When its tiny, precious wings gently touched me,
Its wings looked like they'd drifted down from up high.
But I could see it looked purely terrified.
I told her she's Rosie,
One fine specimen,
She'd been my pet,
I showed her love from within.
I nurtured her till she could be the young mother herself.
I loved my little, sweet butterfly.
She'd been kind the whole time.
I loved her till the very end when she needed to shine.
I wish she could've been her now,
I never should've let her go.
When I solemnly did, I knew it'd been right.
Then she flittered, fluttered into the morning sunlight.

Alice Dowling (12)
The Gregg School, Southampton

MONKEYS

Monkeys stood, shoulders up,
Serving their mistress,
With jugs of coffee,
Still like stone,
Frightened out of their skin,
One movement could bring them hell,
Depression filled their souls.

Abby Hanslip (11)
The Gregg School, Southampton

CLOUDS

Clouds are fluffy and puffy,
Me and my mate spotted one and named the cloud Duffy.
When we look at Duffy she's normally grey,
But when my mate, Jay, and me went to bed,
Strangely, she was red.
We lay there,
We hugged our toy bears,
We thought she was sad and lonely,
Mum came up to say sleep well,
She told us Duffy wasn't lonely,
But she'd been a bad cloud
And turned red.
When we woke up she wasn't there,
There were no clouds anywhere.
We asked Mum why,
She told us there's no need for clouds,
The sun's shining and the sky's blue,
But do you want to play Guess Who?
We watched the hours go by,
No trace of clouds throughout the sky,
Don't know why,
Probably just wanted to say goodbye.

Lillie Bishop (11)
The Gregg School, Southampton

SUNFLOWER

(A Lipogram - E)

Big and bright
Standing atop grass and soil
Shining away through day and night
Like a tall pillar looking upon its world
Until autumn falls and it will too.

Patrick Berry (11)
The Gregg School, Southampton

THE POETRY TRIALS - HAMPSHIRE & SUSSEX

I'M SAVING A SHOT!

I'm saving a shot!
A ball won't go in
I'm saving a shot!
I'm playing to win
If a ball is in my box
I'm as strong as an ox
The ball is in my hands

During a match
I stop an attack
By saving a ball
I'm a brick wall
A man on back post
A man on front post
Working as a group

I'm saving a shot!
A ball won't go in
I'm saving a shot!
I'm playing to win
I'll shout at the lads
To all do a job
A ball won't go in.

Samuel Matthew Jenkins (12)
The Gregg School, Southampton

BE CAREFUL . . .

Four pointy paws,
Dagger-like jaws,
If you go close they'll shut like drawers,
A tail like saws,
He never roars,
A hamster.

Megan Margereson (11)
The Gregg School, Southampton

ONE DARK EVENING …

No moon to show the way,
Oh, how I wish now was day,
Walking along a lonely road,
One dark evening.

A bloodcurdling sound very near me,
My brain is saying, 'Flee, flee, flee,'
I'm running along a lonely road,
One dark evening.

I feel warm air in my ear,
Slowly paralysed in my fear,
I whirl around and here he is,
One dark evening.

I scream and scream, alas, no one hears,
I alone face my fears,
My final endeavour, keep alive,
One dark evening.

Now here I am, my success very clear,
Can I whisper in your ear?
He will find you, I know you know,
One dark evening.

Hannah Creighton (11)
The Gregg School, Southampton

A STORMY SEA

The boat lay on the stormy sea,
As the ship sailed away slowly,
The birds chirped gracefully,
Every day when we all woke,
The sea was wavy,
And the boats in the dock rocked back and forth.

Millie Law (13)
The Gregg School, Southampton

WAR ZONE

(A Lipogram - T)

Bang! Bang! I fell down in pain
Bombs exploding, children crying
In my village, people wonder
Wondering if children have survived
When finally knowing all children are safe
Feeling relieved during dreadful hours

All sunshine disappears, bringing darkness all around
Hiding underground, hoping for peace
When walls fall down and my village is burning
Wishing for hope is all anyone can do
However many people have given up

When children are home and all is well
Happiness comes back and life goes on
For people who remain
For all who died during all wars we will always remember
What you did for us
Peace has improved all around
One day if more people are like you, wars will end.

Rosie Boxall (11)
The Gregg School, Southampton

WOULD YOU LIKE A CUP OF ... ?

If you like a milky brew,
We may have a drink for you
Bagged or loose, Oolong or Chai,
Black, green, lemon, herbal - my!
So many kinds, I see no end,
Perhaps I simply choose a blend!
Grab a cuppa and a scone,
Pull up a chair - ah, jolly bon!
Oh gosh, such clever irony,
How one does love a Rosie Lea!

Mitch Soper (11)
The Gregg School, Southampton

DESTRUCTION

Bang, bang, thud
It ruins walls and hits buildings
Boom, boom, crash
It scars you till you vanish
Thump, thump, wallop
You fall in pain
Tip, top, splash
Our world runs away
Ha, ha, ha
It laughs with might

Bang, bang, thud
Nobody knows about it
Boom, boom, crash
It makes a distinct path
Thump, thump, wallop
No living body backs down
Tip, tap, splash
It's always approaching you
Ha, ha, ha
It talks to you
It is annihilation.

Evelyn Hall (11)
The Gregg School, Southampton

STARS

(A Lipogram - I)

Stars, glow over snowy fields
Stars, glow on the sky
But are shrouded by clouds

Stars, lead lost boats on a dark sky
Stars, guard the sky
But don't always come

Stars, go away at dawn
Stars, to return at dusk
But don't always come back

Stars, concealed by clouds
Stars, may yet glow above
But after hundreds of years of love . . .

Stars, have to end though
Stars, even the purest, pass away
But are born on a dream

Stars, for each new year
Stars, for each who have passed
And to keep hope forever.

Edward Shipley (11)
The Gregg School, Southampton

WW2 WITHOUT ES

(A Lipogram - E)

Loud roar, a colossal wail
Nazi bombs rain down as hail
Alarms cry out, warning our town
Lights out now, blinds drawn down

Rat-a-tat-tat
Rat-a-tat-tat
Rhythmic drumming, alarming sound
Bombs falling all around

'Run Rabbit Run'
Is now sung
Spirits stay high
Nazi aircraft passing us by

All kids play or sit and chat
Many bombs go *rat-a-tat-tat*
Mums worry, looking so forlorn
Praying hard for light of morn.

Elliott Oldrey (11)
The Gregg School, Southampton

RABBITS

(A Lipogram - E)

Fluffy rabbits, pouncing rabbits bouncing up and down.
Charming rabbits, naughty rabbits racing round and round.
Filthy rabbits, shining rabbits, you will want it so.
Baby rabbits, old rabbits looking all about.
Smart bunny, dumb bunny, munching carrots all day long.
Strong bunny, playful bunny, kicking toys across all our rooms.
Girly rabbit, manly rabbit, looking particularly smart.
Worn out rabbit, vigorous rabbit, hoping it's not found.
Wild rabbit, fast rabbit, difficult to catch.
Smooth rabbit, furry rabbit, soft to hold in your hands.

Kaira Feyerabend-Powell (12)
The Gregg School, Southampton

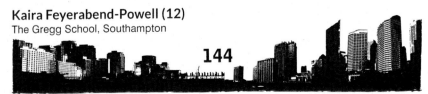

A PARK BENCH

Look, I'm here!
Ponder on me!
I'm freezing cold.

I will burn Sir Armchair, across the park,
Spoiling my view and robbing me of my people!
Now I'm bored and all alone.

I've seen all,
Bird and grass,
I'm wiser - no human knows more.

I have a friend so furry and warm,
He sleeps on me all day long,
Only moves off when his enemy comes.

I wish I could move and help him,
Break gangs - who draw on me!
I am barely really even alive.

Alexander Charlton (11)
The Gregg School, Southampton

SPIDER-PIG

As I walk in by my house
I realise why I am here
Looking high up in the air I see a flying pig
Hovering around my garden
His name was Spider-Pig
Very quickly he zoomed by me
As he headed for my pond
Landing on a lily pad like a plane on a runway
He began searching for food
I knew from then we were going to be friends for life
We lived happily forever
One day in your life you may see a Spider-Pig
Be kind as he may be your good friend.

Jake Smoker (12)
The Gregg School, Southampton

LIPOGRAM WITHOUT A 'U'

The wind is blowing in amongst the trees as little rodents dance and play,
The leaves are whipping everywhere, crackling as they go
And gathering more and more, like a small tornado
Beams of golden light drifting effortlessly inside the swaying trees
The small stream nearby giggling as it races down the creek
Drifting down into a pool with fish darting aimlessly
Swathes of blackberries hanging from their prickly hedge,
With thorns protecting their sweet and refreshing taste
Flowers springing towards the shining star in the sapphire sky
Petals blowing onto the forest floor, creating a soft, feathery blanket
For animals to rest their sleepy and weary heads
In the pond to break the silence frogs croak noisily
Bothering the still afternoon
Foxes are scampering, digging dens and making nests
And then all is peaceful in this place of rest.

Daniel Jones (11)
The Gregg School, Southampton

WHY IS THERE NO T?

Once a lovely dinosaur
His name he said was Dale
Liked munching up paper - or parcels
Or an occasional piece of kale.

He was a very odd dinosaur
A Daleasaurus Rex?
His hands were like bendy chainsaws
Purple scales crisscrossed over his neck!

'A proper name!' his enemies said
'He differs from my friend Rannosaury.
Why look, a piece of bush across his head.
I wish we could nibble him for...
Lunch!'

Will Nelson-Smith (11)
The Gregg School, Southampton

THE POETRY TRIALS - HAMPSHIRE & SUSSEX

NIGHT THINKER

Silent gloom creeps through the room while your eyes begin to close.
Your lungs slow down, there is no sound, the tick-tock of the clock stops.
Tick-tock, tick-tock.

Then in your mind he comes to life, sweeping you off your feet.
The songbirds sing, church bells ring, like snowbells in the sun.
Ding-dong, ding-dong.

But times turn, things occur, everything goes to dust.
There's no time to stop, or you'll go bust, you'll never see light tonight.
Fright-tonight, hold-tight.

Suddenly, you fright, you come to life, your eyes open in shock.
Click!
. . . the night thinker's gone.

Chloe Grace Errington (12)
The Gregg School, Southampton

MY LIPOGRAM

I love to go outside to discover species by my home
But whenever I check the flower beds I find this buried bone
The suspect who is guilty is my terrier who loves to dig
But he is so tiny, so how can he bury this bone which is so big?

The cunning red fox jumps over the fence
He sprints through the weeds so long
He's hunting for some fresh, young hens
But the henhouse lock is strong.

One hedgehog I often see
Which visits us in the night
He's got long, brown, spiky prickles
But will curl up if in fright.

Ollie Mossman (12)
The Gregg School, Southampton

POST DESTRUCTION

Rubble covered the ground,
Smoke greyed the sky,
Scorched bodies lifeless in the street
From the firestorm minutes before.

Thick silence filled the streets,
Not even one house still stood,
Ruins of buildings the only reminder of the once proud town.

Hours before, the town thrived,
Cheerful voices filled the streets.
Now those sounds lie stifled
By the echoes of lost spirits.

The cruel inferno left nothing,
Everything, destroyed.
The fury of the fire prohibited even one soul living.

Paloma Charlotte Hoyos (11)
The Gregg School, Southampton

MUSIC

A man called Max Grin
Like playing a violin

He played all day long
The same boring song

He was a silly bloke
So his violin broke

An awful sin
He mended his violin

He played all day
So his neighbours moved away.

Mark Bowman (11)
The Gregg School, Southampton

THE DRAGON

There once was a wood of tall, oak trees,
In that wood there was a tree,
Beside that tree there was some moss,
Below that moss there was a stone,
Below that stone there was a cave,
In that cave there was an egg,
From that egg there was a crack,
From that crack there was a flame,
From that flame there was a fire,
And from that fire ...
Dragon came.

Isobel Bailey (11)
The Gregg School, Southampton

DREAM

The night enjoyment,
You feel over the moon,
It could be cute or frightening,
There could be witches, gnomes or teddies,
Lovely time with incredible thoughts,
Be strong with frightening thoughts,
Be cheerful the thoughts will come true,
You will consistently get different thoughts,
Enjoy the best moments, you won't think of them next time,
Never tell your thoughts, they won't come true,
So keep your night-time thoughts to yourself.

Eleanor Wright (11)
The Gregg School, Southampton

LOLLIPOPS

A lollipop dream, rarely seen, colours and smell all very well.
Across fields and dales, playgrounds and parks.
A lollipop dream keeps frowns away.
Smile and lick, suck and chew, lemon, lime, purple and blue.
All mixes of flavours, spun in colourful lines,
Red, green and yellow on lips most divine.
Our shop has so many, a rainbow of colour,
Which one shall I have now a challenge I'm sure.
Enjoy a second, never all day, a pole is all remains no sharing for me.
Yummy as can be, enjoyed every day by children begging parents for more.

Ben Cameron (11)
The Gregg School, Southampton

NO T(EA)

Henry had a piece of ham,
Which he placed inside a big, green van.
He drove along a highway long,
Singing loudly a dreadful song.

An enormous dragon smelled his ham
And pounced upon his green ham van.
'Oh no!' cried Henry, 'Oh deary me!
I will have no ham for my . . .
Dinner!'

Henry Earl (11)
The Gregg School, Southampton

THE POETRY TRIALS - HAMPSHIRE & SUSSEX

FROGS AND DOGS

(A Lipogram - T)

Frogs jump and dogs jump,
Frogs swim and dogs swim,
Some frogs live under logs and some dogs jump on logs,
Frogs live in bogs and logs are in bogs,
Some frogs are brown and some dogs are brown,
Some frogs frown and some dogs frown,
Frogs croak while dogs bark,
Big difference!

Paul Lennon Mills (11)
The Gregg School, Southampton

THE FALL

(A Lipogram - O)

The summer came and went
As leaves were flying high
Class was where the children were sent
Plants did wilt and die
The tree branches were bent
Birds were flying in the sky
A chill that we all shall repent
Church bells ringing high
The happy summer is a lament
When warmth is kissed bye-bye
The fall is the prettiest time that is meant
I finish this rhyme with a sigh.

Sarah Hassan (13)
The Gregg School, Southampton

AN AMERICAN LIPOGRAM

(A Lipogram - U)

To help me with this poem I have a clever plan.
I'm going to choose foreign differences and speak American!
I can labor as long as I dare.
I can add color to give it flare.
If it starts to get a little brash,
Well, I'll happily throw it in the trash!

Now, let's take a closer look.
Will that help with this poem? Maybe.
Independent since 1776,
They are practically a baby!
Every object seems to have a different name.
Bear with me and I will explain.
Nappies are diapers and a bonnet is a hood,
There are trash cans, elevators, pitchers and sidewalks.
Got it? Good!

The president is Barack Obama,
He's really calm and can handle the drama!
Their money is dollars and cents,
Everything in the states is big,
One can even say immense!
America has some amazing places for a vacation.
There's Hollywood, New York, San Francisco
And Los Angeles.
All in all, a pretty cool nation!

Madeline Bennett (11)
The Gregg School, Southampton

THE POETRY TRIALS - HAMPSHIRE & SUSSEX

NIGHT SKY

(A Lipogram - E)

I look up into our night sky.
I spot a shocking, gold moon as bright as a million light bulbs.
Colours of a rainbow light up through some woods.
A thousand stunning diamond stars.
Clouds as soft as a pillow, flowing through our sky around a full
moon.
A flash and a spark!
Glowing stars stand out with a twinkling light.
With ominous dark clouds high up and a gloomy, black sky roars.
It throws a gigantic tantrum.
This is our night sky.

Anna Houghton (12)
The Gregg School, Southampton

AUTUMN POEM!

(A Lipogram - E)

The calm brush of autumn winds,
Falling colour brown, gold and black,
Birds fly south for warmth and food,
Sun and warm to chilly and cold.

Twigs falling to damp mud stacks,
Animals put food away for spring,
Long days go to long nights,
Maroon fruit and brown nuts fall and found,
Sun and warm to chilly and cold.

Olivia Munro-Martin (13)
The Gregg School, Southampton

WINTER

(A Lipogram - U)

Snow falling,
Kids calling.

Warm fire,
Christmas choir.

Roast dinner,
Always a winner.

Trees bare,
Misty air.

Cold breeze,
Makes me sneeze.

Warm clothes,
Blocked nose.

Heating on,
Chill has gone.

Georgia Murray (13)
The Gregg School, Southampton

THE POETRY TRIALS - HAMPSHIRE & SUSSEX

FIREWORKS

(A Lipogram - T)

Placed in mud
A firework is ready
Ready for launching up high
A firework launches
Soaring up, up above houses
When suddenly an explosion
A bang, a crash and a pop
Colour is released in mid-air
People look up and are amazed
Amazed by an array of colourful fireworks
People say *ahh* and *ooh* as fireworks explode
Animals are inside, away from loud bangs
Young children go inside and sleep
Displays end, people go home
Skies are a sea of blackness
Big bonfires die down and are now ash
No more fireworks for a year.

Jonathon Duddington (11)
The Gregg School, Southampton

MONSTER

Am I a monster?
Is that what you see?
Please, just stop bullying me!

You always call me nasty names
And you never want to play my games.

Why do you hurt me?
What did I do?
Is it just because I'm smaller than you?

You make me sad and you make me cry,
What's wrong with me?
Just tell me why!

Is it the way I walk?
The way I dress?
The way I talk?

I always see you by that tree,
I'm not that dumb,
I know you're talking about me.

And every time I ask to play,
You always say, 'No, go away!'

I always dread going to school,
Because I know I'll end up feeling like a fool.

I'm always alone,
Sat on the wall,
And think, *why do I have to go to school?*

I can change,
I'll do whatever you say,
Please, for once, just let me play.

Am I a monster?
Is that what you see?
Please, just stop bullying me!

Fifi Palmer (11)
The Henry Beaufort School, Winchester

THE POETRY TRIALS - HAMPSHIRE & SUSSEX

A CREATION OF FRIENDSHIP

The first day she saw you,
She smiled then got butterflies.
She tried to talk but her voice disappeared,
For all he knew she was invisible.

The second day she saw you,
She knew she had to make a move.
She thought about it all day,
Then she knew what to do.

The third day she saw you,
She filled his locker full of roses,
Wrote her name and waited for a reply,
It took all day but nonetheless it came.

The fourth day she saw you,
People were throwing roses and laughing.
She knew it was because of her,
She had to do something.

The fifth day she saw you,
She apologised and told everyone the truth.
They knew they shouldn't laugh or joke,
She wanted it to stop and for them to be friends.

The sixth day she saw you,
She held his hand and smiled.
People sat with them, they were being friendly,
They had parties, laughs and fun.

The seventh day she saw you,
It was in their secondary school.
There were laughs and tears,
But that is just life!

Remember, friends are forever,
Keep them close and you'll never lose.

Rebecca Jane Tan (11)
The Henry Beaufort School, Winchester

THE INEVITABLE ILLUSION

We all live yet we cease to exist.
We all lose yet fail to reminisce.
When we fall the dust becomes home but even with this
We are never alone.
There comes a moment when the truth may be told.
We are only a fading shadow
Amongst a wave of those who are dauntless and bold.
How strange it seems that those who are poor
Obtain nothing in this world more than paper.
The authentic millionaires own little
Yet their benevolence pays more than what life may offer.
I am neither great nor small.
I laugh and cry, that's the truth of it all.
I am scared of the dark and the ghouls beneath my bed
Although I realise these thoughts are only in my head.
Society is a cage of which nightmares are created.
One dream may be wished but soon it shall be defeated.
We are ridiculed for what we wear,
The shape of our body and the length of our hair.
If we do escape this master race,
We are certain to be thrown back into our place.
We are based on work ethic rather than compassion.
We are told to figure out equations
Rather than a real life situation.
We are encouraged to create our own tale
Yet told that imagination will only cause us to fail.
From the moment you're born, your world should be your oyster.
How can we do this if society has already planned our future?
These statements are complicated yet so very truthful.
You have to break the mould.
Your life won't be lethal.
I am neither fat nor skinny.
I am neither quiet nor whiny.
My hair is short yet I am a woman.
Society forgets that we are only human.
Do what makes you happy rather than 'normal'.
Choose your own journey whether it be casual or formal.
Even if you can't decide a path there is no need to stress.

THE POETRY TRIALS - HAMPSHIRE & SUSSEX

See how your life pans out and only do your best.
Now there is only one thing you must keep in mind:
Stars all need darkness if they are to shine.

Ines Mazdon Delas (14)
The Henry Beaufort School, Winchester

POPPIES BLOOMED!

Let the brave ones stand
Proud and tall
But wishing to be anywhere but there
Down in the trenches
Up on the fields
As the poppies bloomed, crimson

Rattling gunfire
Beating hearts
And cries of anguish
As the poppies bloomed scarlet

Finally victory comes
But victory with its prize
A price the brave ones paid
Paid with their life
While the poppies bloomed ruby

And those who waited
Are still waiting for the brave ones to return home.
Tears meandered in the swelling streams of hope
Until they were rivers of sorrow
While the poppies bloomed red

But the sorrow passed
And the funerals finished memorials stood proud and tall
The world had changed, unlike ever before
And the poppies grow crimson.

Holly Marshall (11)
The Henry Beaufort School, Winchester

WINTERTIME

I hear the wind rustling through the air,
Although it's chilly, I do not care.
Different colours merge through my hair,
At different times of the year.

My arms hold children when they play,
Helping to keep the sadness away.
The boys and girls keep me company every day,
I have never felt bad that way.

My body is strong and wide,
Protecting my heart safe inside.
People hug me all the time,
When they do my emotions chime.

My legs help me stand and grow tall,
Without them I wouldn't be here at all.
They are long and winding,
They swirl and are intertwining.

I am home to many a creature,
All of which I love and preciously nurture.
Lots of visitors come and go,
Most are friends that I know.

I see new life every year,
This lovely moment is so dear.
These young creatures which I cherish,
Without me they would perish.

Now it's time for us to sleep,
And escape to the winter keep.
I can't wait until spring is here,
It is when we all reappear.

My life is just simply to be,
Just like an absolute fantasy.

Eliot Liversidge (12)
The Henry Beaufort School, Winchester

THE POETRY TRIALS - HAMPSHIRE & SUSSEX

FAMILY!

Family is the main thing you need,
To learn from,
To learn how to to speak,
Family is your stepping stone to life,
If you had no family what would you do?

We all have family,
Without family what would you do?
We all know what family feels like,
Even if you don't remember them,
The stepping stone to life is your family.

Family brings you to new places,
They pay for your needs,
Celebrate your birthday,
Family lets you be you,
Anything you need, they will be there.

We are all lucky to have a family,
Family helps you through the hard times,
Bring you to preschool,
Then to primary school,
Then to secondary and to college and university.

We all need family for all our needs,
They don't care if you lose a race,
They love you no matter what,
They will help you with what you need,
We have to have family.

Family looked after you when you were down,
We all support each other,
You share together and live together,
Your parents are like your guardian angels,
Family is your stepping stone to life.

Keian John Offord (13)
The Henry Beaufort School, Winchester

BLITZ A-Z ACROSTIC POEM

A ir raid siren moans in the dead of night.
B ombs start cascading down from German bombers.
C ries of citizens struck down by rubble pierce the air.
D rones from the dozens of aircraft make the ground shudder.
E normous buildings crumple to the ground.
F lames lick up the sides of shops and terraces.
G as and water explodes out of the road.
H avoc erupts as a bomb hits a public shelter.
I n London the sky is orange with the glow of fire.
J unkers peal off from the bomber squadrons and swoop low, machine guns blaring.
K illing starts every time a wave of bombers flies over.
L egs of dead women and children litter the dark road.
M others try to soothe their screaming children.
N o one dares to think what would happen if a bomb landed on them.
O pening bomb hatches, scattering bombs onto . . . well they don't care.
P etrified children whimper among the noise.
Q uivering air raid wardens keep turning the siren, hoping for an all-clear to sound.
R aids happen on houses while everyone is in the shelters.
S pitfires fly down onto the bombers from clouds of smoke.
T ension is high in the shelters.
U nderground stations stink with the smell of soot, sweat and dirty nappies.
V IPs shelter in Windsor Castle watching the orange sky and listening to the booms of bombs.
W hite charcoal flakes of massive beams.
X -ray machines burn in the hospitals that were not meant to be bombed.
Y ellow fire erupts within incendiary bombs.
Z eppelin-like barrage balloons stops the Junkers from dive bombing.

Oscar Edward Thompson (11)
The Henry Beaufort School, Winchester

THE POETRY TRIALS - HAMPSHIRE & SUSSEX

A SHADOW OF A MEMORY

The day you left still haunts me
When you left us all alone
The world became dark and daunting
Wishing for you to return home

Your ghost casts an ominous shadow over my heart
One of tedious longing and sorrow
Grief has torn my heart apart
Like there's never a tomorrow

You lay pale like my wedding dress
On a pristine hospital bed
Your rasping breaths still tortures my mind
Your last words echo in my head

I remember treading water in the sorrow that engulfed me
Panic etching an irreversible pattern on my heart
But you fell limp too soon, letting me drown for I had nothing to fight
for
I wish I could turn the clocks back, back to the start

No one understands
I don't expect them to
But I wish you were here to comfort me
For I have nothing else to do

I try to let go of your shadow
But no matter how much I try
No matter how much I scold myself
I can only hear your voice: 'Please don't cry!'

Memories are painful
But having none is more painful still
Your last words are what I hold you to:
'I'll always love you . . .'

Laura Arnott (11)
The Henry Beaufort School, Winchester

HOPE

He felt afraid
His life was delayed
Just silence all the time
As years passed by
Little did he know that someone was out there
Heart and soul to wear

One day a voice spoke
One of the sweet, old folk
With no cash to spare
And barely any clothes to wear
Just a bit of food
The man was in a good, old mood

Just for today
He gave it away
The sun starting to set
The folks own pet
The old man's soul
And a little foal

His heart in a place
Never to waste
The time came
For his fame
Out in the open
His heart not to be broken.

Alice Little (11)
The Henry Beaufort School, Winchester

MY DEARLY LOVED FRIEND

Dear, My Best Friend,
I wish I could see you for one last time,
I miss you,
If only I could hold you for one last time,
I miss you,
I need you,
I am so sad without you,
Please come home,
Please,
I was in tears,
I needed you,
I still need you,
No one can replace you,
No one,
You were my best friend,
You still are,
You will always be in my heart,
I will never forget you,
Please come back,
I need you,
I will always love you,
Goodbye Speedie,
My dearly loved hamster.

Amy Justine Offord (12)
The Henry Beaufort School, Winchester

A FRIEND AND A LOVER

Gentle and kind,
You're on my mind,
Sure and strong, don't mind being wrong,
So alive and aware, you always care,
Open and true,
You help when I am blue.
Friend and lover, you will always be true.

Tia Burgin (14)
The Henry Beaufort School, Winchester

THE TALE OF THE DEER

Bang, bang, bang, he was all alone.
Days passed all quiet,
There was no early song,
He felt so alone,
All life felt gone.
He had to find help,
The other world called,
He would try and succeed,
But all he did was fall.
He stepped into the city,
The buildings were tall,
The cars screeched so loud,
Bang, he was gone.
His head hung low,
His faced soaked with sweat,
He fell to the floor,
And the floor's where he slept.
He never got up,
He lay with his mum,
In the world of the dead,
And that's where the last song was sung.

Betsy Harvey (11)
The Henry Beaufort School, Winchester

SAKURA

A sakura tree
Hunches over sadly, as
Her last blossom falls.

In the far distance,
People are unaware of
The tree's loneliness.

Astha Subba (12)
The Henry Beaufort School, Winchester

WAR

When the talk of war was still kindling,
And the worries of what were to confront us were young,
The thought of war appealed to me - heroism, glory, victory,
But with one simple letter, those thoughts were none,
It wasn't play anymore, this was hard, this was true
And this was war . . .
Blood, sweat, fear,
Quick, sharp breaths,
Hardly hear,
Sudden death,
Apprehension brewing,
Sticky, sweaty hands,
Clenched around the forsaken,
Now it's my turn;
Bang, bang
There is no tale to hide this beast,
No sequins can cover up those gaping holes,
No words will talk their way out of the pain,
The scenes play over. And over again
The memory will stay, like a leech on flesh,
The memories will always stay.

Rohan May (13)
The Henry Beaufort School, Winchester

THE 'I AM' POEM

I am happy and exhausted,
I wonder if I will get good grades in school.
I hear the swift sounds in the trees,
I see the ocean in a bag under my eye.
I want to be rich so I can share the money with others,
I am a bad football player and a keen Xbox gamer.
I pretend to be the best artist even though I'm not,
I feel excited because Christmas is coming.
I touch the stars in the clear night sky,
I worry about the future and what will come.
I cry when I think about my aunt, who is dead,
I am a creature of God and Jesus.
I understand that not everyone can get what they want in life,
I say that dreams can come true.
I dream that I will be the best architect in the UK,
I try to be the best person I can be.
I hope I win this competition, or come close,
I am Ben Elkins, a boy from Basingstoke.

Ben Elkins (12)
The Henry Beaufort School, Winchester

AMAZING ANIMALS

Have you ever heard,
The sounds in the jungle?
Screeches of a bird,
Or a lion's tummy rumble?

The swaying of the trees,
Where the monkeys leap
And the buzzing of the bees,
Which makes it hard to sleep!

Have you ever seen
An elephant's trunk?
And where the sloths lean
On a jungle tree trunk?

When the night-time comes,
The loud snores start,
All these amazing animals,
Will never grow apart.

Ellena Lousie Cable (12)
The Henry Beaufort School, Winchester

FRIENDS

A friend is always there for me,
They let me be myself,
They'll always stand up for me,
And care about my health.
They're friendly, loyal and warm inside,
Like a fire that will never hide.
They never insult or judge your opinion,
And are like a helpful minion.
They're easy to trust
And won't treat you like a speck of dust.
They treat you like the way you want to be treated
And are never conceited.
They always give you a lot of support,
And don't care whether you're fat, thin, tall or short.
You're never sad when you're with them
And they're as precious as a gem.

Hannah Louise Woodhall (11)
The Henry Beaufort School, Winchester

BLUE

Blue is the colour of the sky,
A bit like blueberry pie.

Blue is the colour of candyfloss at fairs,
You can also see the colour blue in people's hair.

Blue is a piece of bubblegum going pop!
It is also the colour of a giant blue lollipop.

Blue is one of the colours of our great British flag,
It is also the colour of a designer bag.

Blue is the colour of the big, blue sea,
It is also a royal colour for everyone to see.

Blue is a clichéd colour for what boys wear,
But it is always a colour for everyone to share.

Megan O'Neill (13)
The Towers Convent School, Steyning

THE POETRY TRIALS - HAMPSHIRE & SUSSEX

BLUE

What do you think of when you hear the word 'blue'?

A bright, bold, sunny sky,
Or a deep, dark, stormy sea.

A cold, cruel, trickling tear,
Or a delicate, dancing, blooming bluebell.

What about the tone?

Light blue is happy and joyful,
Like a child opening a magical gift.
It can be calm and relaxed too,
Like a baby, unstirred in its cosy crib.

Dark blue,
However,
Is evil and sinister,
Like a master criminal,
A partner in crime.

It can also
Be sad and depressed,
Like a mourning mother
Missing her loved one.

Blue.
Beautiful blue.
First prize ribbon,
Dazzling kingfisher.

Blue was always there.
Looking down on us from the sky,
Staring up at us from the sea.

What do you think of when you hear the word 'blue'?

Megan Viljoen (13)
The Towers Convent School, Steyning

RED

Red.
As kind as the gentle touch of rose petals,
As sharp as the hottest burning flames of fire.

Deceiving and sinister,
Sweet betrayal.
Blood spills and yells,
'Soft monstrosities.'

Warm and soft,
Lovingly sweet and true.
A juicy, red berry,
Overflowing with purity.

And just like that,
With the flip of a hat,
From evil to innocent,
From bad to good.

Red is the colour,
A colour of passion and peace.
Red is the colour,
A colour of anger and scorn.

Red is where we begin,
The deepest loving souls.
Red is where we die,
Our heart's beating ceases.

As kind as the gentle touch of rose petals,
As sharp as the hottest burning flames of fire.
Red.

Jemima Coleman (14)
The Towers Convent School, Steyning

RED CANVAS

We paint the world,
It's our blank canvas,
Staring back at our reflection,
Colour is warped, colour is perception.

Red: how can one describe it?
Connotations so distant,
But look a little deeper,
Open your mind a little further,
They may be closer than you think.

Red: a colour that says,
I love you.
Red: a colour that says
Danger - don't say I didn't warn you.

Take a rose, a sign of hope,
Of love everlasting.
A red rose for the one you love,
Scattered with thorns, hidden warnings.

Crimson; the deep blood red,
The colour of fairy tales,
Little Red Riding Hood, Snow White,
Both tales of poison struck with spite.

Now you see the deeper meaning,
The one you never saw,
Red of the primary spectrum,
Colour is warped.

Francesca Blondell (13)
The Towers Convent School, Steyning

CROSSWORD COLOURS

Contrast within dimensions,
burning retentions,
any labels
for any perceptions.

Like a cake,
that you bake,
many layers within,
what you make.

Different ideas,
making it clear,
that what you see,
isn't what you hear.

Imaginative ways,
to let your mind stray,
like ever-changing waves,
on a hot, sunny day.

So isn't it absurd,
that no one has heard,
that someone's favourite colours,
come from a crossword?

Ella Savage (13)
The Towers Convent School, Steyning

BLACK

Black is the colour of all things bad
It is the colour of darkness and everything sad
You may argue, you may disagree
But black is bad in my mind you see

Black drags you down from your glorious tone
So that you feel miserable, skin through bone
This hideous colour is darker than shadows
At night black terrorises the villages and meadows

So now I've convinced you! Black is cruel!
But did you ever consider breaking Black's rule
Blackcurrants juicy are my favourite fruit
Snow White's hair? Or James Bond's suit?

Black can be marvellous like a starry sky
Black is the colour of a magpie's eye
Think of the luck a black cat brings
Think of the song a blackbird sings

So now it is up to decide
Will black make you laugh?
Or will black make you cry?

Freya West (13)
The Towers Convent School, Steyning

BLUE AND RED

Blue is sea and sky and sadness -
Red is wildfire and war and warning.

Blue is calm, peaceful, bliss,
Red is hatred, flame, hot.

When cold nips at your fingertips,
When bright lights burn through your eyelids.

Blue is icy water,
Red is a love heard.

Flame and ice,
Fire and water.

Georgia Howarth (13)
The Towers Convent School, Steyning

NEWBORN COLOURS

Pink, a colour attached to girls,
Like cotton candy, oh so dandy.

Rosy, flushed, glowing,
All words used to describe
A feeling of warmth.

Blue, oh such a lovely colour,
It makes me think of being in a summer haze.

The calm waves against the shore,
Oh, how I wish I could see more!

Maddi Scarborough (13)
The Towers Convent School, Steyning

Est. 1991

YOUNG WRITERS INFORMATION

We hope you have enjoyed reading this book – and that you will continue to in the coming years.

If you're a young writer who enjoys reading and creative writing, or the parent of an enthusiastic poet or story writer, do visit our website www.youngwriters.co.uk. Here you will find free competitions, workshops and games, as well as recommended reads, a poetry glossary and our blog.

If you would like to order further copies of this book, or any of our other titles give us a call or visit **www.youngwriters.co.uk**.

Young Writers
Remus House
Coltsfoot Drive
Peterborough
PE2 9BF

(01733) 890066
info@youngwriters.co.uk